1��7

BODY SYSTEMS:
ANATOMY AND PHYSIOLOGY

MACMILLAN
HEALTH
ENCYCLOPEDIA

1

BODY SYSTEMS:
ANATOMY AND PHSYIOLOGY

MACMILLAN PUBLISHING COMPANY
NEW YORK

MAXWELL MACMILLAN CANADA
TORONTO

MAXWELL MACMILLAN INTERNATIONAL
NEW YORK   OXFORD   SINGAPORE   SYDNEY

EDITORIAL CREDITS

Developed and produced by
Visual Education Corporation, Princeton, NJ

Project Editor: Darryl Kestler

Editors: Richard Bohlander, Susan Garver,
Michael Gee, Emilie McCardell,
Cynthia Mooney, Suzanne Murdico,
Frances Wiser

Editorial Assistant: Carol Ciaston

Photo Editors: Maryellen Costa, Michael Gee

Photo Research: Cynthia Cappa, Sara Matthews

Production Supervisor: Anita Crandall

Proofreading Management: Amy Davis

Art Editors: Maureen Pancza, Mary Lyn Sodano

Advisor, Anatomical Illustrations:
David Seiden, Ph.D.
Robert Wood Johnson Medical School
Piscataway, New Jersey

Layout: Maxson Crandall, Lisa Evans

Word Processing: Cynthia Feldner

Design: Hespenheide Design

The information contained in the *Macmillan Health Encyclopedia* is not intended to take the place of the care and advice of a physician or health-care professional. Readers should obtain professional advice in making health-care decisions.

PHOTO CREDITS

Jacket: Howard Sochurek/The Stock Market

A. Paul Bowling: 78 (top), 78 (bottom)

PhotoEdit: Bill Aron, 29; Robert Brenner, 9, 25 (left); Amy Etra, 54; Myrleen Ferguson, 6 (right), 25 (middle); Tony Freeman, 25 (right); Richard Hutchings, 45; David Young-Wolff, 6 (left)

Photo Researchers: Michael Abbey, 91 (bottom); M. Guthrie/Biology Media, 91 (top)

Martin M. Rotker: 15, 20, 50

Macmillan Publishing Company
866 Third Avenue
New York, NY 10022

Maxwell Macmillan Canada, Inc.
1200 Eglinton Avenue East, Suite 200
Don Mills, Ontario M3C 3N1

Macmillan Publishing Company is part of the Maxwell Communication Group of Companies

Printed in the United States of America

printing number
1   2   3   4   5   6   7   8   9   10

Library of Congress Cataloging-in-Publication Data

Macmillan health encyclopedia.
    v. <1–   >
    Includes index.
    Contents: v. 1. Body systems—v. 2. Communicable diseases—v. 3. Noncommunicable diseases and disorders—v. 4 Nutrition and fitness—v. 5. Emotional and mental health—v. 6. Sexuality and reproduction—v. 7. Drugs, alcohol, and tobacco—v. 8. Safety and environmental health—v. 9. Health-care systems/cumulative index
    ISBN 0-02-897439-5 (set).—ISBN 0-02-897431-X (v. 1).—ISBN 0-02-897432-8 (v. 2).
    1. Health—Encyclopedias.   I. Macmillan Publishing Company.
RA776.M174   1993
610′.3—dc20   92-28939
                                                        CIP

Volumes of the *Macmillan Health Encyclopedia*

1 *Body Systems* (ISBN 0-02-897431-X)
2 *Communicable Diseases* (ISBN 0-02-897432-8)
3 *Noncommunicable Diseases and Disorders* (ISBN 0-02-897433-6)
4 *Nutrition and Fitness* (ISBN 0-02-897434-4)
5 *Emotional and Mental Health* (ISBN 0-02-897435-2)
6 *Sexuality and Reproduction* (ISBN 0-02-897436-0)
7 *Drugs, Alcohol, and Tobacco* (ISBN 0-02-897437-9)
8 *Safety and Environmental Health* (ISBN 0-02-897438-7)
9 *Health-Care Systems/Cumulative Index* (ISBN 0-02-897453-0)

The *Macmillan Health Encyclopedia* is a nine-volume set that explains how the body works; describes the causes and treatment of hundreds of diseases and disorders; provides information on diet and exercise for a healthy lifestyle; discusses key issues in emotional, mental, and sexual health; covers problems relating to the use and abuse of legal and illegal drugs; outlines first-aid procedures; and provides up-to-date information on current health issues.

Written with the support of a distinguished panel of editorial advisors, the encyclopedia puts considerable emphasis on the idea of wellness. It discusses measures an individual can take to prevent illness and provides information about healthy lifestyle choices.

The *Macmillan Health Encyclopedia* is organized topically. Each of the nine volumes relates to an area covered in the school health curriculum. The encyclopedia also supplements course work in biology, psychology, home economics, and physical education. The volumes are organized as follows: 1. *Body Systems: Anatomy and Physiology;* 2. *Communicable Diseases: Symptoms, Diagnosis, Treatment;* 3. *Noncommunicable Diseases and Disorders: Symptoms, Diagnosis, Treatment;* 4. *Nutrition and Fitness;* 5. *Emotional and Mental Health;* 6. *Sexuality and Reproduction;* 7. *Drugs, Alcohol, and Tobacco;* 8. *Safety and Environmental Health;* 9. *Health-Care Systems/Cumulative Index.*

The information in the *Macmillan Health Encyclopedia* is clearly presented and easy to find. Entries are arranged in alphabetical order within each volume. An extensive system of cross-referencing directs the reader from a synonym to the main entry (GERMAN MEASLES see RUBELLA) and from one entry to additional information in other entries. Words printed in SMALL CAPITALS ("These substances, found in a number of NONPRESCRIPTION DRUGS . . .") indicate that there is an entry of that name in the volume. Most entries end with a list of "see also" cross-references to related topics. Entries within the same volume have no number (See also ANTI-INFLAMMATORY DRUGS); entries located in another volume include the volume number (See also HYPERTENSION, 3). All topics covered in a volume can be found in the index at the back of the book. There is also a comprehensive index to the set in Volume 9.

The extensive use of illustration includes colorful drawings, photographs, charts, and graphs to supplement and enrich the information presented in the text.

Questions of particular concern to the reader—When should I see a doctor? What are the risk factors? What can I do to prevent an illness?—are indicated by the following marginal notations: Consult a Physician, Risk Factors, and Healthy Choices.

Although difficult terms are explained within the context of the entry, each volume of the encyclopedia also has its own GLOSSARY. Located in the front of the book, the glossary provides brief definitions of medical or technical terms with which the reader may not be familiar.

A SUPPLEMENTARY SOURCES section at the back of the book contains a listing of suggested reading material, as well as organizations from which additional information can be obtained.

GLOSSARY

acute   Refers to a symptom or disease that begins suddenly, is usually severe, and generally lasts a short time.

agent   A substance or force that can bring about a certain biological, chemical, or physical change.

anatomy   The study of the structure, organs, and various components of the human body.

antibiotics   A group of drugs, produced from certain bacteria and fungi, that are used to treat a wide variety of bacterial infections (see ANTIBIOTICS, 7).

bacteria   (sing. *bacterium*) Single-celled, microscopic organisms, abundant in living things, air, soil, and water. Some are beneficial to humans, while others cause disease (see MICROORGANISMS, 2).

behavior   The way a person acts and responds to the environment.

bloodstream   The blood flowing through the veins, arteries, and capillaries.

blood vessels   A general term for the arteries, veins, and capillaries through which blood circulates in the body.

cartilage   Strong, dense, elastic tissue found in the nose, ears, and joints (see CONNECTIVE TISSUE).

catalyst   A substance that speeds up a chemical reaction without being changed or destroyed by the action.

cavity   An area of decay in a tooth caused by bacteria; also, a hollow area inside the body, such as the chest cavity.

chronic   Refers to a disorder or set of symptoms that persists over a period of time or recurs frequently. Asthma and hypertension are chronic conditions.

congenital   Refers to a characteristic or condition that is present before or at birth but is not necessarily inherited from parents.

degenerative disease   A long-term disease that involves a gradual breakdown of the structure and function of tissues and organs. It is a condition that usually worsens with time.

dependency   The physical or psychological reliance on something, such as on drugs or alcohol.

diagnosis   The process by which a physician identifies a disease or disorder.

disease, disorder   An abnormal change in the structure or functioning of an organ or system in the body that produces a set of symptoms. The change may be caused by infection, heredity, environment, or lifestyle or by a combination of these.

genetic   Refers to a characteristic, condition, or disease that is transmitted to an individual through the genes of one or both parents (see GENETICS, 6).

health   The physical, mental, and social well-being of a person. Health is not just the absence of disease.

health care   Techniques and procedures concerned with the promotion and maintenance of health, the prevention of illness, and the treatment of disease.

heredity   The traits—physical, mental, and emotional—that children receive from both of their parents by means of genes; also, the process by which such traits are transmitted by genes.

immunity   The body's ability to protect itself from disease.

infection   A condition caused by bacteria, viruses, fungi, or other microorganisms that invade and damage body cells and tissues.

infectious   Refers to a disease that can spread (see COMMUNICABLE DISEASE, 2).

inflammation   Redness, swelling, pain, and heat in a body tissue due to physical injury, infection, or irritation.

involuntary   Refers to body functions and actions over which a person has no control.

life span   The length of an individual life.

lifestyle   The way a person lives, as shown by attitudes, habits, and behavior.

membrane The thin layer of tissue that lines body cavities, divides organs, or forms a boundary between individual cells.

organ A part of the body made up of specialized tissues that are used for a specific function. The heart and eyes are organs.

organism Any plant or animal.

pain A feeling of discomfort—slight or severe—caused by an injury, disease, or functional disorder.

physiology The study of the processes, activities, and functions of the body.

preventive care Health care that emphasizes good diet, exercise, immunizations, and regular checkups as ways of avoiding health problems or diagnosing them earlier.

protein A nutrient needed for the growth, repair, and regulation of the body (see PROTEINS, **4**).

pulmonary Pertaining to the lungs.

risk behavior An action, such as smoking or not wearing a seat belt, that increases the likelihood of injury or illness.

stress The body's response to any physical or mental demand made on it.

symptom A change in normal body function indicating the presence of a disease or disorder. A sore throat is a symptom of infection.

vascular Pertaining to the blood vessels and the circulation of blood through the body.

virus The smallest known living infectious agent (see MICROORGANISMS, **2**).

wellness A state of physical, mental, and social well-being that allows a person to function at his or her best.

ABDOMEN

The abdomen is the body cavity that extends from the CHEST (thorax) to the lower PELVIS. Surrounding the cavity are the back muscles and spine at the rear and three layers of abdominal muscles in the front and on the sides. These muscles support the abdominal organs. They also allow you to bend and turn your upper body. The abdominal cavity is lined by a thin membrane called the peritoneum, which also covers the organs within.

Inside the abdomen are the *stomach*, LIVER, *large and small intestines*, PANCREAS, GALLBLADDER, KIDNEYS, and *bladder* (see illustration: The Abdomen). A woman's abdomen also contains her uterus and ovaries, and a man's abdomen includes his prostate gland. The abdomen is sometimes called the *solar plexus*, but this term actually refers to a network of nerves within the abdomen.

Because the front and sides of the abdomen are not protected by bone, the abdomen is vulnerable to injury. If you have ever been hit in the stomach and lost your breath, you probably know just how vulnerable the area is.

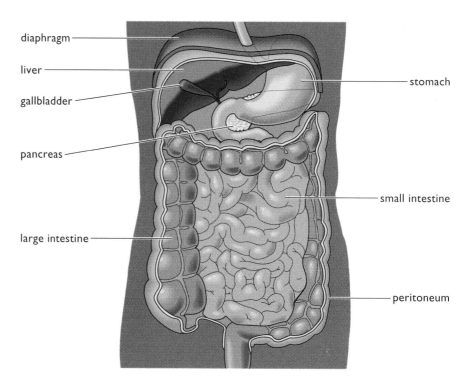

diaphragm

liver

gallbladder

pancreas

large intestine

stomach

small intestine

peritoneum

The Abdomen.

ADENOIDS

The adenoids are two masses of infection-fighting tissue located at the back of the nasal passage and above the tonsils (see illustration: Location of the Adenoids). Part of the LYMPHATIC SYSTEM, the adenoids act as filters to prevent germs from entering the body through the NOSE. In early

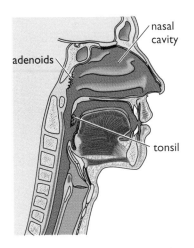

Location of the Adenoids. *The adenoids are at the back of the nasal passages.*

childhood, when upper respiratory infections are common, the adenoids swell. By about age 4 or 5, they usually shrink to the size of almonds, and by puberty, they often nearly disappear.

Adenoid Problems and Treatment In some cases, a child's adenoids do not shrink and may even grow larger. When this happens, the adenoids may block the passage between the nose and the throat. This causes chronic snoring, breathing through the mouth, and a buildup of mucus in the nasal passage. The adenoids may also block the eustachian tube (the passage between the middle ear and the throat), which can result in repeated ear infections and hearing loss. In addition, enlarged adenoids may prevent secretions from the nose and sinuses from draining properly.

While an infection involving the adenoids usually responds well to antibiotics, repeated infections may necessitate an adenoidectomy, the surgical removal of the adenoids. (See also RESPIRATORY SYSTEM; SINUS.)

ADOLESCENCE

Adolescence is the transitional period between childhood and adulthood. It is a time when people undergo significant physical and emotional growth. Adolescence corresponds roughly to the teenage years, but it can begin sooner and end later in many cases. Adolescents are frequently preoccupied with the physical changes that are taking place in their bodies. They are also busy shaping their own personalities and identities. Many people have their first real experience with independence, responsibility, love, and sex during adolescence.

Physical Changes *Puberty* is the period when a person's reproductive system begins to function. The PITUITARY GLAND begins to secrete hormones that bring about the development of certain traits that are characteristic of each sex. Puberty usually begins about 1 or 2 years earlier for girls than for boys. Typically, girls enter puberty around age 10 or 11 and complete the process by age 15 or 16. Many boys do not begin puberty until age 12 or 13 and may continue to undergo physical changes until they are 17 or 18.

In boys, the sexual characteristics that develop during puberty include the enlargement of the penis and testes; the growth of pubic, body, and facial hair; a deepening of the voice; and an increase in muscle mass in the shoulders, thighs, and biceps. In girls, changes in sexual characteristics include the development of breasts; the growth of pubic and body hair; and the addition of fat around the hips, buttocks, and breasts. Girls also experience *menarche*, the onset of *menstruation*, usually between ages 11 and 13. Just before menarche or within 1 or 2 years, girls begin ovulating and are then capable of becoming pregnant and having a child. For both boys and girls, these sexual changes are usually accompanied by great spurts of growth until adult height and weight are achieved.

Emotional Changes The production of sex hormones may result in emotional upheaval as well as physical growth. Adolescents begin to

Adolescence. *During adolescence, both young men and young women are very concerned with their appearance and the physical changes taking place within their bodies. Many teenagers experience sexual feelings and love for the first time. Adolescence is also the period when most people begin to form their own attitudes and opinions.*

experience sexual feelings. Hormonal changes can cause episodes of moodiness, exhilaration, depression, and apathy. Teenagers feel emotions such as love or rejection very intensely. This is due partly to increased hormone levels and partly to the fact that they are experiencing those emotions for the first time.

Adolescence is a time for experimentation. Teenagers begin to form their own attitudes and opinions, which may differ from those of parents and teachers. At the same time, they are under intense pressure to conform to the behavior, values, and lifestyles of their friends. Conflicts with authority figures such as parents are very common. During this period of experimentation and rebellion against adult values, adolescents sometimes adopt extreme hairstyles and clothing fashions. Some also experiment with tobacco, alcohol, and other drugs. Some adolescents become sexually active in their middle or late teens. People who are homosexual usually discover this sexual orientation during adolescence. However, for some teenagers homosexual behavior may be experimental and temporary.

Adolescents should be aware of the physical and psychological changes that are taking place in themselves. They need to understand that emotional turmoil, confusion, and self-doubts are normal, if unsettling, aspects of the process of becoming an adult. Parents and adolescents should try to keep the lines of communication open so that parents can understand their children's problems and help them cope with the changes they are experiencing. (See also PEER PRESSURE, 5; SELF-IMAGE, 5; FEMALE REPRODUCTIVE SYSTEM, 6; MALE REPRODUCTIVE SYSTEM, 6; PUBERTY, 6.)

HEALTHY CHOICES
●●●●●●●●●●●●

▶ **ADRENAL GLANDS** The adrenal glands (or suprarenal glands), part of the ENDOCRINE SYSTEM, are two small masses of tissue located on top of the kidneys. Each adrenal gland is like a miniature chemical factory; together, these glands produce a number of hormones that affect almost every system in your body. Like all glands of the endocrine system, adrenal glands release hormones directly into the bloodstream.

Structure of the Adrenal Glands Each adrenal gland has two distinct parts: the adrenal cortex and the adrenal medulla (see illustration:

Location and Structure of the Adrenal Glands). The outer portion, the *adrenal cortex,* is stimulated by a hormone from the pituitary gland. The adrenal cortex produces hormones that help maintain the balance of certain chemicals that affect the body's METABOLISM. One of these, *aldosterone,* regulates the chemical balance of the blood. It does this by stimulating the kidneys to absorb sodium and water and to excrete potassium. Another group of hormones plays a role in the processing of nutrients for body cells. For example, these hormones help the liver convert fat and glycogen into glucose, a substance the cells use for fuel. These hormones have two additional functions: they reduce inflammation and help the body deal with stress. Small quantities of the sex hormones (androgens and estrogens) are also produced in the adrenal cortex. These may play a role in adolescent sexual development.

The inner part of the adrenal gland, the *adrenal medulla,* is part of the *sympathetic nervous system.* In times of danger or stress, a part of the brain sends nerve messages that stimulate the adrenal medulla to produce a hormone called epinephrine. EPINEPHRINE (also known as adrenaline) and another hormone, *norepinephrine,* cause the heart to beat faster, the passageways in the lungs to expand, and the blood supply to the muscles to increase. These changes, known as the fight-or-flight response, enable the body to react more efficiently to stress or danger. The amount of epinephrine in the bloodstream usually diminishes quickly after the body has coped with a threat.

Disorders of the Adrenal Glands   Diseases of the adrenal glands are rare but can be very serious when they do occur. *Addison's disease* is a gradual decline in the production of certain adrenal hormones. Untreated, the disease may lead to acute adrenal failure, which can be life-threatening.

Cushing's disease is the opposite of Addison's disease. In *Cushing's disease,* the adrenal glands produce too great a quantity of certain hormones. This disease is usually caused by tumors on the adrenal gland that stimulate the cortex to overproduce hormones. Both diseases can be controlled by medication or, in the case of tumors, by removal of the tumor or the entire adrenal gland. People whose adrenal glands have been removed must remain on medication for the rest of their lives. (See also NERVOUS SYSTEM; STRESS, **5.**)

Location and Structure of the Adrenal Glands.   *Each adrenal gland has two distinct parts: the adrenal cortex and the adrenal medulla. The adrenal cortex secretes hormones that affect body metabolism, blood chemicals, and sexual development. The adrenal medulla produces hormones, most notably epinephrine, that help the body deal with danger and stress.*

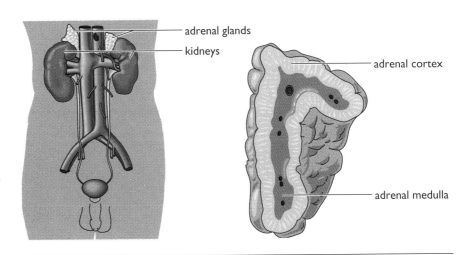

adrenal glands

kidneys

adrenal cortex

adrenal medulla

▶ **ADRENALINE** see EPINEPHRINE

▶ **ADULTHOOD**

Adulthood is the period of life that follows ADOLESCENCE. For most people, adulthood is the longest stage of life, spanning the years between the age of about 18 or 19 and death. A person entering adulthood has grown to full height and has reached sexual maturity. During this period, the adult gradually becomes aware that the aging process is having an effect. Adulthood is generally considered to have three stages: early, middle, and late. Each stage is marked by many physical, emotional, and social changes common to almost all adults.

Early Adulthood In early adulthood, between the ages of 18 or 19 and 24, most people leave their parents' home and become independent. This is the stage in which a majority of young adults complete their formal education or job training and start a career. Lifestyles are also chosen at this time. Choices related to such matters as diet and exercise can affect health and general well-being throughout life. Romantic relationships often result in stronger commitments than was the case earlier. Many people get married during this period in their lives. The body usually remains relatively unchanged during early adulthood.

Middle Adulthood Middle adulthood is generally regarded as spanning the years between 25 and about 59. During this stage, running a household and bearing and rearing children are major priorities, but divorce and remarriage are not uncommon. This may also be a time of advancing in a career, changing careers, or—for some parents—reestablishing a career, as well as planning for eventual retirement. Also, social relationships are often most numerous at this stage. Toward the latter part of middle adulthood, many parents face the experience of their children leaving home. At about the same time, some people must turn their attention to their own parents, who may need help in dealing with diminished physical abilities, illness, and even death.

Physical changes are more noticeable in this period. Women experience menopause; wrinkles begin to appear; skeletal muscles begin to lose strength. Although most individuals in middle adulthood remain healthy and energetic, some have health problems and slow down appreciably. Such differences may be caused by hereditary and environmental factors.

> During late adulthood, aging is accepted as a normal process of life. Late adulthood is the stage of retirement for most people.

Late Adulthood From age 60 on, responsibilities become fewer and AGING is accepted as a normal process of life. Late adulthood is the stage of retirement for most people. Some find this a difficult adjustment, while others regard retirement as an opportunity to do the things they have always wanted to do but never had time for. Many people must face the loss of a spouse, partner, or friends during late adulthood. On the other hand, grandchildren or other children often enrich the lives of older adults, providing them with a sense of joy and hope for the future.

The effects of aging are obvious during late adulthood. Stiffer joints, less efficient organs, and slower reactions are common. Yet, increasingly, many people are physically and mentally active well into their eighties and beyond. (See also LIFESTYLE, 4; HEREDITY AND ENVIRONMENT, 5.)

▶ AGING

Aging. *Many older adults find they have the time to become involved in community activities.*

HEALTHY CHOICES

The body goes through certain physical and mental changes as it progresses through the normal human life span. During this aging process, the body's organs become less efficient and physical performance declines to some extent. Older people often have chronic illnesses or disabilities. For many people, aging is an unwelcome experience. But aging has benefits as well. Older people can draw on a lifetime of experience in dealing with life's problems and crises. Once their children are grown, older people usually have fewer responsibilities and more time to enjoy themselves.

Physical Changes   The average life span in the United States is about 75 years. As a person's body approaches the end of its life span, organs and tissues begin to deteriorate. At some point after the age of 40, the skin becomes less elastic, causing wrinkles to appear, the muscles lose bulk, and the heart becomes less efficient. Many people become somewhat farsighted and require glasses for reading and close work. Many also experience some hearing loss.

Psychological Changes   Some people worry about memory loss and declining intelligence as they grow older, but few elderly people experience a significant loss of mental function. The brain does lose nerve cells over the years, and this causes a slowing of reaction time and some minor memory lapses. Although the sex drive changes as people age, older adults can remain sexually active and enjoy a satisfying sex life.

Chronic Illnesses   Certain diseases commonly afflict the elderly. These *diseases of aging* include heart disease and arteriosclerosis. The heart muscle becomes less efficient in pumping blood, while the blood vessels become less elastic and increasingly clogged with fatty tissue that restricts blood supply. *Diabetes* is one of the most common diseases of aging. It is caused by the failure of the pancreas to regulate blood sugar, but in most cases it is controllable. Millions of older adults suffer from arthritis, the wearing away of joints and bones, and osteoporosis, the loss of calcium in the bones. Alzheimer's disease is a degeneration of the brain that affects about 10 percent of those over 65.

Heredity is the most important factor in determining how long people will live and what diseases of aging they may contract. However, people can do a great deal to ensure themselves a long and healthy life regardless of their genetic makeup. Avoiding smoking and drinking alcohol, following a nutritious, low-fat diet, and exercising regularly may increase longevity. A good mental attitude is also helpful. The elderly should try to stay active, be tolerant and patient, maintain ties with friends and families, and seek out new experiences. (See also LIFE EXPECTANCY; DIABETES, 3; GENETICS, 6; MENOPAUSE, 6.)

▶ ANKLE

The ankle is the JOINT between the leg bones and the foot. It is a *hinge joint* that allows the foot to move up and down. The ankle works with your feet as well as your knee and hip joints to enable you to walk and run.

In the ankle joint, the lower ends of the shinbones, the *fibula* and *tibia,* fit over the top of the *talus,* the uppermost bone of the foot (see illustration: Bones of the Ankle). The outer edge of the ankle is supported by the fibula. Several strong *ligaments* crisscross the joint, holding the bones of the legs and foot in place. The ligaments prevent the bones from moving sideways and help you maintain your balance. You can feel your *Achilles tendon* at the back of your ankle. It is the largest tendon in the body, connecting the muscles of the calf to the heel bone. The Achilles tendon helps lift the heel of the foot and pull the toes down with each step.

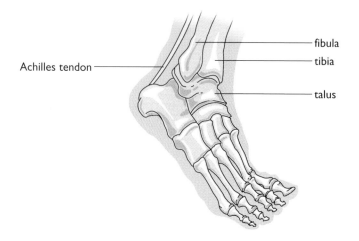

Achilles tendon —

— fibula
— tibia
— talus

Bones of the Ankle.

Common Ankle Injuries and Disorders   A sprained or twisted ankle is the most common injury. It usually occurs when the foot is twisted over its outside edge, overstretching the ligaments on the outside of the ankle. A minor sprain can be treated by the RICE technique (rest, ice, compression, elevation). A more serious sprain with torn ligaments may require a cast or splint; sometimes the injury needs to be repaired surgically. People who are prone to ankle injuries may find it useful to wear elastic ankle supports when exercising or participating in sports. Swelling in the ankles can occur if you do a lot of standing, particularly in hot weather. Occasionally, swollen ankles are symptomatic of other disorders such as rheumatoid arthritis, heart disease, poor circulation, gout, and varicose veins. Elevating the legs and wearing support stockings will help reduce the swelling. (See also CONNECTIVE TISSUE; MUSCULOSKELETAL SYSTEM.)

► **ANUS**

The anus is the outlet at the end of the *alimentary canal,* or digestive tract, through which feces, semisolid waste composed of undigested material and water, pass out of the body. An extension of the RECTUM, the anus is about $1\frac{1}{2}$ inches (about 4 cm) long. Two layers of sphincter muscles keep the anus closed except during defecation, the expulsion of feces from the body. The internal sphincter muscle is involuntary, that is, not under a person's control. The external sphincter muscle, however, can be relaxed at will to allow defecation.

Disorders of the Anus The most common problem of the anus is *hemorrhoids*. These are enlarged blood vessels under the lining of the walls of the anus that result from severe pressure during defecation. In extreme cases, hemorrhoids may be surgically removed. Straining to expel feces may also result in tears or fissures to the anal walls. These usually heal themselves. Itching caused by infection or pinworm infestation is easily treated.

A digital exam of the anus, feeling the area with a gloved finger, may help a physician locate and diagnose certain anal problems. In a more extensive procedure known as proctoscopy, the physician uses an internal viewing tube to see the area. Sometimes a biopsy, or tissue sample, is taken as well. (See also HEMORRHOIDS, **3**.)

▶ AORTA

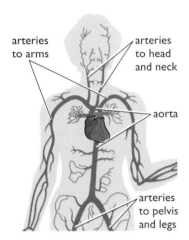

arteries to arms

arteries to head and neck

aorta

arteries to pelvis and legs

The Aorta and Its Major Branches.

The aorta is the longest and largest ARTERY in the body. It is responsible for supplying oxygen-rich blood to body tissues and organs. The blood supply of the whole body passes through the aorta, which is about 1 inch (2.5 cm) in diameter at its point of origin. The aorta begins at the lower left chamber of the HEART, arches up and over the heart, and descends through the chest and abdomen. At the top of the arch, the aorta branches into four main smaller arteries that carry blood to the head, neck, and arms. In the abdominal area, the aorta divides into two main arteries that supply the pelvis and the legs with blood (see illustration: The Aorta and Its Major Branches).

Fatty deposits may narrow the opening of the aorta, as well as other arteries, eventually causing the wall to thicken and harden, a condition known as *atherosclerosis*. This, in turn, may lead to *hypertension*, the rupture of an artery, or a number of circulatory problems. (See also CIRCULATORY SYSTEM; ATHEROSCLEROSIS, **3**; HYPERTENSION, **3**.)

▶ APPENDIX

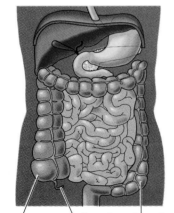

cecum   appendix   large intestine

Location of the Appendix.

The appendix is a short, thin tube that projects downward from the cecum, the beginning of the large intestine (see illustration: Location of the Appendix). The position of the appendix may vary slightly from person to person. The appendix is about 3.5 inches (9 cm) long in adults and has a lining that is similar to the lining of the intestine. The appendix has no known function in humans.

The appendix is commonly thought to be left over from a time when all people were vegetarians. Its enclosure is the perfect breeding ground for the bacteria that early people needed to digest vegetable fibers. Now, a large amount of lymph tissue in the appendix helps prevent bacteria trapped there from causing infection.

Occasionally, however, the appendix does become infected and inflamed, a condition called *appendicitis*. Anyone who experiences pain in the lower right corner of the abdomen should consult a physician. In severe cases of appendicitis, the appendix is removed surgically. (See also APPENDICITIS, **3**.)

▶ ARTERY

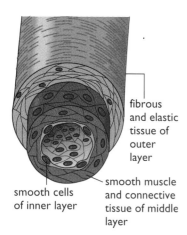

fibrous and elastic tissue of outer layer

smooth muscle and connective tissue of middle layer

smooth cells of inner layer

Structure of an Artery.
Arterial walls are elastic, and they expand and contract with each heartbeat. This action aids the heart in pumping the blood through the body.

Arteries are blood vessels or tubes in the CIRCULATORY SYSTEM that carry blood pumped away from the heart to all parts of the body. There are two kinds of arteries. By far the most numerous, *systemic arteries* carry bright-red, oxygen-rich blood from the lower left part of the heart, through the AORTA, the body's largest artery, to all parts of the body except the lungs. The *pulmonary arteries* carry brownish, oxygen-poor blood from the lower right part of the heart to the lungs.

Structure of the Arteries   The walls of the arteries are composed of three layers. The inner layer is made up of smooth cells, the middle layer of muscle and connective tissue, and the outer layer of fibrous tissue (see illustration: Structure of an Artery). Because the arterial walls are both thick and elastic, the arteries are able to expand with each heartbeat as the blood courses through them and then contract between heartbeats. This action assists in moving the blood along.

Artery Disorders   A major cause of death in the United States, *athero-sclerosis* is an artery disease caused by a buildup of fatty tissue on the inner wall of the artery. As a result, blood flow to specific parts of the body may be restricted or even completely blocked. An *aneurysm,* a throbbing, balloon-shaped swelling on the arterial wall, may be caused by a thickening and hardening of the wall, by high blood pressure, or by infections. If an aneurysm ruptures, it can cause severe blood loss. (See also ATHERO-SCLEROSIS, **3**; HYPERTENSION, **3**.)

▶ BLADDER

see URINARY TRACT

▶ BLOOD

Blood is the fluid that circulates in the veins and arteries. It consists of blood cells and a yellowish liquid called *plasma*. Blood's primary function is to deliver *oxygen* and nutrients to cells and to take away *carbon dioxide* and other wastes. It also plays a role in the body's defense against injury and infection. Finally, the blood carries hormones and other messengers to different parts of the body.

The Makeup of Blood   The body of an average adult contains about 10 pints (about 5 L) of blood. Approximately half of this volume is made up of cells; the rest is plasma. Most of the blood cells are red blood cells, which outnumber white blood cells by almost 700 to 1. Blood also contains cell fragments called platelets. Blood volume is continually renewed, as old or damaged cells are replaced by new blood cells. Most new blood cells are produced by specialized cells located in bones, although some types mature elsewhere in the body. Old cells are broken down; some parts are reused and others are excreted from the body.

The Functions of Blood Components   *Red blood cells (erythrocytes)* carry oxygen from the lungs to the body's cells by providing a container

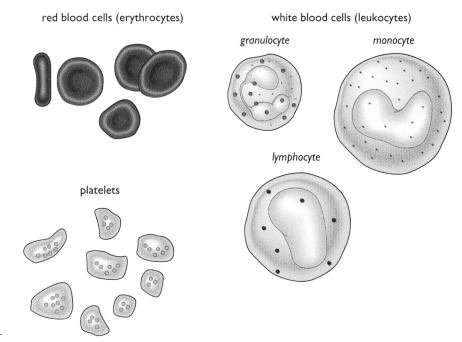

red blood cells (erythrocytes)

white blood cells (leukocytes)

granulocyte

monocyte

lymphocyte

platelets

Blood Cells. *In addition to the red blood cells, blood contains three types of white blood cells—granulocytes, monocytes, and lymphocytes—and platelets, which help repair blood vessels.*

for a protein called hemoglobin. *Hemoglobin* binds with oxygen molecules in the lungs. Then, as the hemoglobin travels through the bloodstream, it discharges oxygen to the cells that need it and picks up carbon dioxide. Oxygen-rich hemoglobin gives blood its red color.

White blood cells (leukocytes) are an important part of the body's defense system (see IMMUNE SYSTEM). There are three main types of white blood cells. The first type, *granulocytes,* are concerned primarily with isolating and killing invading bacteria. They also play a role in controlling allergic reactions. The second type, *monocytes,* also kill foreign matter. These include very large cells called *macrophages,* which swallow foreign matter along with dead cells. The third type, *lymphocytes,* focus on specific bacteria or viruses. One kind of lymphocyte, the *B cell,* forms antibodies that attack specific viruses and bacteria. Another kind of lymphocyte called a *T cell* attacks foreign and abnormal cells (see illustration: Blood Cells).

When you cut yourself or when a blow ruptures blood vessels inside your body, blood flows freely until the platelets begin their work. The main function of *platelets* is to repair injured blood vessels. When platelets encounter an injured blood vessel, they become sticky and clump together. This plugs the holes in blood vessels, stopping the flow of blood. Platelets then release chemicals that initiate *blood clotting* and cause the blood vessels to contract.

Plasma, the fluid in which blood cells and platelets travel through the body, also carries dissolved chemicals, including proteins, hormones, nutrients, and waste products. The proteins play a key role in the clotting process begun by the platelets. Through a series of chemical reactions, these proteins help produce long fibrous threads that form the webbing of a blood clot. Plasma from which these proteins have been removed is called *serum.* (See also BLOOD CLOT, **3.**)

Blood Problems Disease can affect any of the blood's components. Anemia results when the body does not produce enough red blood cells. In leukemia, the body produces too many white blood cells and they do not mature properly. HIV, the virus that causes AIDS, damages the T-cell lymphocytes so that they cannot defend the body from disease. A variety of bleeding disorders, including hemophilia, result from a lack of platelets or any of the clotting chemicals. Uncontrolled bleeding, caused by one of these disorders or by injury, can be treated with blood transfusions. Too much of some clotting chemicals can cause blood to clot too readily, contributing to circulatory disease. (See also AIDS, 2; HIV, 2; ANEMIA, 3; HEMOPHILIA, 3; LEUKEMIA, 3.)

HEALTHY CHOICES
●●●●●●●●●●●●

How to Prevent Problems While some blood diseases are inherited, many can be avoided through lifestyle choices. A diet sufficient in iron and vitamin B_{12} will help ensure that your red blood cells function properly. If you do not smoke, your hemoglobin should carry oxygen effectively. You can lower your risk of abnormal blood clotting by avoiding oral contraceptives. You can also learn how and where to apply pressure to stop bleeding from a wound. (See also BLOOD PRESSURE; BLOOD TEST; BLOOD TYPE; BLEEDING, 8.)

▶ BLOOD BANK

A blood bank is a place that collects, tests, stores, and distributes blood for transfusion. Large-scale blood storage began in 1937, after the development of refrigeration and a substance that keeps the blood from clotting. Even with today's technology, blood can't keep forever. Refrigerated blood lasts for no more than 35 days.

Blood banks determine the BLOOD TYPE and Rh factor of donated blood and also screen blood for the presence of disease. If a donor is accepted, 1 unit (450 mL) of blood is drawn from a vein in the donor's arm. It can be stored as whole blood or separated into parts by spinning test tubes filled with blood at high speed until the parts form separate layers. This process makes it possible to give people only the blood parts they need.

Located in hospitals and regional or community agencies, blood banks are usually run by the American Red Cross or by members of the American Association of Blood Banks. These groups distribute the blood where it is needed. The Food and Drug Administration (FDA) regulates the nation's blood banks. In recent years, the FDA has paid special attention to the procedures blood banks use to screen blood for HIV, the virus that causes AIDS. Through effective screening HIV can be kept out of the nation's blood supply. (See also BLOOD TEST; RH FACTOR, 6.)

▶ BLOOD PRESSURE

Blood pressure is the force of blood flowing against the artery walls. Blood pressure rises and falls in concert with the cycle of the HEART. Maximum pressure, or *systolic pressure,* occurs at the moment that the heart is actually pumping blood. Like the liquid in a funnel, which pools until it can drip through the small hole, blood stays in the arteries

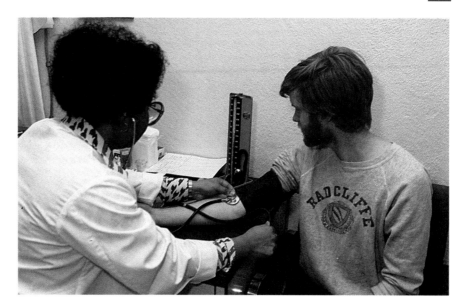

Measuring Blood Pressure.

until the smaller blood vessels can absorb it. This creates pressure in the arteries. Healthy arteries can expand under this pressure, keeping systolic pressure within normal ranges. When the heart rests between beats, blood pressure lessens accordingly and at this phase is called *diastolic pressure.* Normal diastolic pressure indicates that the heart is really resting between beats.

How Blood Pressure Is Measured   Blood pressure is measured with an instrument called a *sphygmomanometer* (SFIG moh muh NAHM ut ur). An inflatable cuff is wrapped around the arm, just above the elbow. As the cuff is inflated, it temporarily stops the flow of blood. At this point, the physician or other health-care worker may place the listening piece of a stethoscope on the inside of the arm, just at the edge of the cuff, and should hear no sound since the flow of blood has been cut off. As the cuff is gradually deflated, the blood flow resumes and can be heard. At the same time, the sphygmomanometer gauge shows the systolic pressure. The cuff is then further deflated until the sound disappears, indicating that the pressure is dispersed. Now the gauge shows the diastolic pressure. Typical blood pressure measurements are shown as fractions, with the systolic pressure above the diastolic pressure. Normal blood pressure for young adults is approximately 110/75 (expressed as "one-ten over seventy-five").

Blood Pressure Problems   When blood pressure is high, the heart must work harder to pump blood against that pressure. *Hypertension* is consistently high blood pressure. Over time, this can damage the heart and blood vessels as well as other organs. The treatment of hypertension may include changes in the diet and lifestyle of the patient and, in some cases, medication.

How to Prevent Problems   Certain health habits will help you lessen the chances of developing hypertension. These include controlling your weight, maintaining a diet low in salt and fat, exercising regularly, and, if possible, avoiding drugs such as oral contraceptives that cause blood pressure to rise. Finally, because stress and high blood pressure have been

HEALTHY CHOICES
●●●●●●●●●●●●

linked, you need to learn ways to cope with and reduce stress in your life. These lifestyle choices are especially important if you have a chronic illness such as diabetes or a family history of hypertension or if you are pregnant. These factors will raise your risk of developing high blood pressure. (See also ATHEROSCLEROSIS, **3**; HYPERTENSION, **3**.)

RISK FACTORS
▶ ▶ ▶ ▶ ▶ ▶

▶ BLOOD TEST

Blood tests analyze a sample of blood to help assess a person's overall state of health or the function of specific body systems. Such tests can focus on the blood's components, on the chemicals it contains, or on any germs that may be present. This information is often vital in diagnosing diseases of the blood, heart, and other major organs, as well as infections such as mononucleosis.

Types of Tests   Tests that analyze the components of the blood look at the number, shape, size, and appearance of cells and may also examine the blood's clotting function. One series of tests of this type, the *complete blood count (CBC)*, provides an overview of all these factors. The CBC can be used to detect *anemia* or to indicate the possible need for other types of tests. (See also ANEMIA, **3**.)

The second group of blood tests focuses on chemicals in the blood. These chemicals may come from the food you eat or from drugs and other substances you ingest. For example, the amount of sodium (salt) or lipids (cholesterol) in a blood sample can be measured. These tests are also used to check blood for the presence of drugs ranging from aspirin to alcohol.

Finally, blood can be analyzed for the presence of *microorganisms* such as bacteria and viruses. Tests in this group are sometimes called blood *cultures* because a sample of blood is left to culture, or grow, before the results are read.

> Blood tests analyze a sample of blood to help assess a person's overall state of health or the function of specific body systems.

Testing Procedures   Blood tests require a small sample of a patient's blood, usually drawn from a vein near the bend in the elbow. The physician or technician first cleans the skin with an antiseptic and then ties a rubber hose called a constricting band around the arm above the elbow. Sometimes the person being tested is asked to form and release a fist. Both the constricting band and the flexing of the hand force blood into the vein, making it easier to find. A needle is inserted and blood is withdrawn into a container called a syringe. If arterial blood is required, it is drawn from the wrist or groin. When only a few drops of blood are needed, they are drawn by pricking the fingertip with a sterilized instrument called a lancet.

Analysis   Laboratories perform the blood analysis. Some laboratories use computerized analyzers that can perform and interpret several tests on a single sample. The test results are compared to a range of normal results established by the laboratory performing the analysis. Although many precautions are taken to ensure accuracy, errors in test results do sometimes occur. For this reason, any abnormal test results will usually be tested several times to confirm their accuracy. (See also BLOOD TYPE; MICROORGANISMS, **2**.)

▶ **BLOOD TYPE**

Human BLOOD is divided into four types and four subtypes according to the presence or absence of certain substances. Some of these blood types (or groups) are not compatible with one another, and mixing them can cause medical problems. The system of classifying blood makes it possible to match blood donors and recipients safely.

All human blood contains plasma, cells, and dissolved chemicals. But it is the presence or absence of proteins called *antigens* that characterizes the different blood groups. Your blood is type A, B, AB, or O depending on whether it contains A antigens, B antigens, both A and B antigens, or neither A nor B antigens. Your blood is also either Rh positive (Rh+) or negative (Rh−), depending on whether it contains the *Rh factor,* another group of antigens. (See also ANTIGEN, **2.**)

Some blood types can be mixed, while others cannot (see chart: Blood Type Compatibility). For example, type A has anti-B antibodies. If the two are mixed, these antibodies will cause type B blood to clump, a process called *agglutination,* which can cause serious problems. It is therefore crucial to determine a person's blood type before giving that person a blood transfusion. Type O blood is often called the universal donor because it can be given safely to people with type A, B, and AB blood of the same Rh factor.

Rh− blood does not contain anti-Rh antibodies unless it has been exposed to Rh+ blood. For example, when an Rh− woman carries an Rh+ baby, her blood may form antibodies against the baby. Today, women who are Rh− can avoid this problem by taking a prescribed medication. (See also BLOOD TRANSFUSION, **3**; RH FACTOR, **6.**)

Blood type of recipient

Blood type of donor	AB	A	B	O
AB	◯	✕	✕	✕
A	◯	◯	✕	✕
B	◯	✕	◯	✕
O	◯	◯	◯	◯

◯ = compatible   ✕ = incompatible

Blood Type Compatibility.

▶ **BONE**

Bones are the hard, rigid structures that make up the *skeleton,* the framework that provides shape to the body and enables it to move. The adult human body contains 206 bones. Bones are made up of calcium, phosphorus, and water held together by a fibrous protein called *collagen.* Bones generate blood cells, protect internal organs, support the muscles and skin, and store important minerals. Although they are rigid and seemingly unchanging, bones are living structures whose cells are being repaired and replaced constantly in a process known as *ossification.*

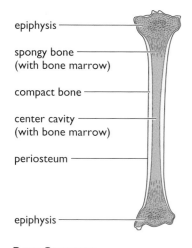

epiphysis

spongy bone
(with bone marrow)

compact bone

center cavity
(with bone marrow)

periosteum

epiphysis

Bone Structure.

Bone Structure   There are two types of bone tissue: dense, compact tissue and spongy tissue. The long bones of the body, found in the arms and legs, consist largely of compact bone, while the flat bones, the ribs and skull, are mainly spongy bone.

A typical bone (see illustration: Bone Structure) has a membranous surface called the periosteum, which contains nerve cells and blood vessels. Below the periosteum is a hard shell of compact bone encasing spongy bone. The spongy bone is a mesh of calcium and hollow areas filled with bone marrow. BONE MARROW, which generates red and white blood cells, also fills the hollow central cavity in long bones. At each end of the long bones is the *epiphysis* (ih PIF uh sus), an area of bone and cartilage where growth takes place during childhood and adolescence.

Bone Disorders   Bones are subject to fracture and to several diseases. A broken bone must be set in its normal position and held in place until it heals. Vitamin D deficiency causes *rickets* in children and *osteomalacia* in adults. These diseases soften and deform the bones. *Osteomyelitis* is an inflammation of the bone caused by bacteria. Millions of older adults are afflicted with *osteoarthritis*, a wearing away of the bones at the JOINTS. In addition, many older adults, primarily women, suffer from *osteoporosis*, a disease that causes the bones to lose calcium so that they become brittle and break easily. Bone cancer is a malignant growth that replaces bone.

Maintaining Healthy Bones   To develop and maintain strong bones, you should eat calcium-rich foods, such as dairy products, and leafy, dark-green vegetables. Regular exercise, such as walking, swimming, and jogging, helps strengthen bones and builds bone mass. Because loss of the hormone estrogen (a natural chemical substance) after menopause is believed to be the major cause of osteoporosis, many physicians recommend that women consider estrogen replacement therapy after menopause. (See also MUSCULOSKELETAL SYSTEM; ARTHRITIS, **3**; OSTEOPOROSIS, **3**.)

BONE MARROW   Bone marrow is soft, fatty tissue found in the hollows of bones. Bone marrow produces all the body's red blood cells and platelets and most of its white blood cells. When BLOOD flows through the marrow, it picks up new blood cells to replenish those that have been lost.

The bones of children contain red bone marrow. As children mature, red marrow is replaced by yellow marrow in the long bones of the arms and legs. In adults, only the bones of the skull and torso contain red marrow. Red marrow produces the red blood cells and the platelets that are necessary for clotting. Yellow marrow produces some of the white blood cells.

Life-threatening diseases can develop when the bone marrow produces too many or too few blood cells. Aplastic anemia, a condition that occurs when bone marrow produces too few blood cells, causes severe infections and bleeding. Physicians usually treat aplastic anemia with blood transfusions and antibiotics. In some types of leukemia, a large number of abnormal white blood cells are produced in the bone marrow. This, too, causes severe infections and bleeding and can be fatal. A bone marrow transplant is a procedure in which healthy bone marrow is used to replace diseased marrow. Such transplants are sometimes used to treat potentially fatal cases of aplastic anemia and leukemia. (See also ANEMIA, 3; LEUKEMIA, 3.)

▶ BRAIN

The brain is the master controller of the NERVOUS SYSTEM. It is responsible for conscious thought, memory, learning, sensations, movement, language, personality, and emotions. It also monitors and regulates body functions such as heartbeat, breathing, and sleep. The functions of the brain are very similar to those of a computer. It takes in information from the outlying parts of the body and from the body's surroundings, then processes that information and sends instructions back to the appropriate muscles or sense organs (such as skin and eyes).

The brain is a soft, grayish organ covered with ridges or folds (see illustration: Cross Section of the Brain). Located in the skull, it is protected by the skull bones, membranes, and fluid that fills the spaces between the membranes. The brain of a newborn weighs about 1 pound (about 0.5 kg). By the time the child is 6 years old, the brain has grown to its full size and weighs approximately 3 pounds (about 1.4 kg).

Structure and Function of the Brain The human brain is an enormously complex organ consisting of about 100 billion nerve cells called NEURONS. The brain and the SPINAL CORD make up the central nervous system. Nerve pathways extend from the brain down the spinal cord and out through the peripheral nerves to all parts of the body. The sense organs send information, in the form of electrical impulses, along the nerve pathways to the brain. The information is then interpreted by one of the three major structures of the brain: the brain stem, the cerebellum, or the cerebrum (see illustration: Major Parts of the Brain).

Brain Stem The bottommost structure, the brain stem, connects the brain with the spinal cord. It controls vital functions, such as breathing, and coordinates incoming information from throughout the body. The brain stem is composed of three substructures: the medulla, the pons, and the midbrain. The *medulla* controls heartbeat, breathing, blood pressure, vomiting, swallowing, and coughing. Located just above the medulla is the *pons*, which is the Latin word for "bridge." It is made up of nerve fibers and acts as a pathway for many nerve impulses to and from various parts of the brain. The pons also assists the medulla in controlling breathing. The *midbrain*, which is above the pons, connects the cerebrum with other parts of the brain and with the spinal cord. The nerves in the midbrain help control eye movements and some hearing reflexes (such as turning the head to better hear a sound).

Deep within the brain, at the top of the brain stem, are the thalamus and the hypothalamus. The *thalamus* relays sensory information from other parts of the nervous system to the covering of the cerebrum. The HYPOTHALAMUS enables the nervous system to communicate with the glands of the ENDOCRINE SYSTEM. The hypothalamus helps regulate body temperature, as well as appetite, some emotions, and the sex drive.

> The brain stem connects the brain with the spinal cord. It controls vital functions, such as breathing, and coordinates incoming information.

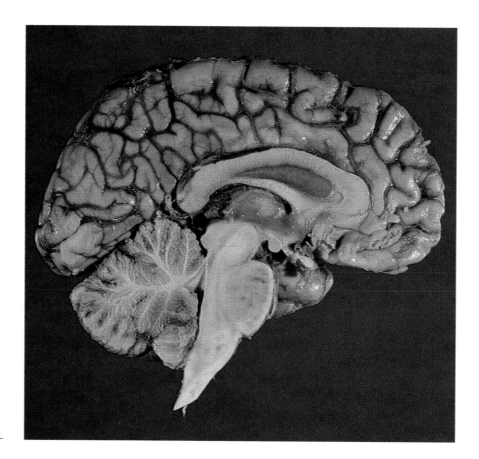

Cross Section of the Brain.

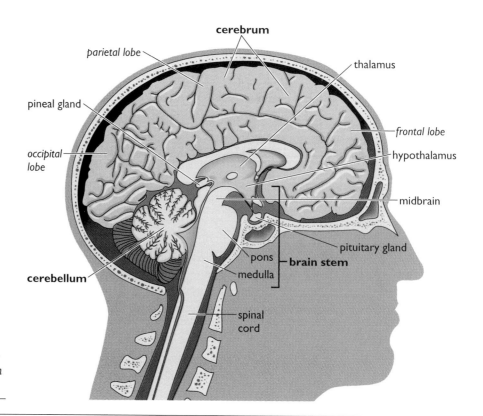

cerebrum

parietal lobe

thalamus

pineal gland

frontal lobe

occipital lobe

hypothalamus

midbrain

pituitary gland

pons

brain stem

medulla

cerebellum

spinal cord

Major Parts of the Brain. *In this view, half of the brain is cut away to show structures normally covered by the cerebrum. The temporal lobe, the lower, outside part of the cerebrum (located at the ear), is not visible in this view.*

20

BODY SYSTEMS: ANATOMY AND PHYSIOLOGY

Cerebellum   The cerebellum sits behind the brain stem. It is a large mass of nerve tissue that is divided into halves, or hemispheres. The cerebellum is responsible for coordinating muscle movement and maintaining the body's balance and posture. The functions of the brain stem and cerebellum take place without conscious awareness or thought. (See also PINEAL GLAND; PITUITARY GLAND.)

Cerebrum   The cerebrum is the uppermost and by far the largest structure of the brain. It produces reasoning, sensation, awareness, imagination, memory, and language. The cerebrum is divided into left and right hemispheres, which are mirror images of each other. The major sensory and motor nerve paths between the brain and the rest of the body cross as they pass through the brain stem. For this reason, each side of the cerebrum controls motor and sensory actions of the opposite side of the body. Some higher-level activities, however, are controlled by one hemisphere. For example, it is believed that the right hemisphere is the center for creative ability and that the left hemisphere controls math ability.

> The cerebrum produces reasoning, sensation, awareness, imagination, memory, and language. It is divided into left and right hemispheres, which are mirror images of each other.

Each hemisphere of the cerebrum is covered by a *cerebral cortex*, a coating of gray matter where incoming information is analyzed. It is in the cerebral cortex that very complex actions—decision making, speech, writing, and creative thought—actually begin. The surface of the cerebrum is made up of coils of nerve cells called convolutions, which are separated by grooves. Each hemisphere of the cerebrum is further divided into four lobes: the *frontal, parietal, temporal,* and *occipital*. Each lobe controls certain specific activities, such as sight (occipital lobe), hearing (temporal lobe), touch (parietal lobe), and movement (frontal lobe).

Disorders of the Brain   The most common brain disorder is a cerebrovascular accident. This disorder, commonly known as a *stroke*, occurs when blood supply is cut off to part of the brain or when a blood vessel bursts in the brain, causing massive clotting. Symptoms of stroke depend on which part of the brain is damaged, but they can involve partial paralysis, loss of speech, blurred vision, and mental confusion. More generalized brain damage may occur when the brain is deprived of oxygen for more than a few minutes.

A hard blow can cause the brain to swell inside the skull, resulting in headaches, amnesia, depression, paralysis, convulsions, and slurred speech. These symptoms usually disappear as the brain tissue heals, but severe injuries can cause permanent damage. (See also ALZHEIMER'S DISEASE, 3; CEREBRAL PALSY, 3; PARKINSON'S DISEASE, 3; STROKE, 3.)

▶ CAPILLARY

Weaving through all the tissues and organs of your body, capillaries are the smallest and most fragile vessels that carry blood. Capillaries link the smallest arteries to the smallest veins. The main job of the capillaries is to bring nutrients such as oxygen and glucose to body cells and tissues and to carry away carbon dioxide and other waste products. The diameter of a capillary is only slightly greater than that of the blood cells that pass through it. Its thin walls allow the nutrients and waste products to pass through.

Blood flow through a capillary is controlled by a ring of muscle found at its end. Capillaries open and close according to the needs of an organ or tissue. For example, when you are playing the piano, all the capillaries in your hands are open to blood flow. When your hands are still, many of the capillaries in them are closed.

Capillaries also help regulate body temperature. The opening of skin capillaries brings blood to the skin's surface, making you appear flushed and feel warmer. When skin capillaries close, blood is diverted and the skin becomes paler and cooler.

Capillary Injury   A fall, a bump, or a sharp blow can break capillaries under the skin's surface, causing blood to leak into surrounding tissues. This may result in swelling and discoloration as in a "black" eye or "black and blue" contusion or bruise. (See also CIRCULATORY SYSTEM.)

► CARTILAGE   see CONNECTIVE TISSUE

► CELL

muscle cells

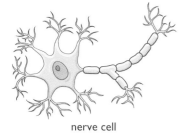

nerve cell

Types of Cells.

A cell is the smallest unit of living matter that can exist independently. All living things are made up of cells. Some plants and animals, such as bacteria and protozoa, are one-celled organisms. Most species of plants and animals are made up of large numbers of cells that assume different, specialized forms to carry out specific body functions. The human body contains trillions of cells.

Each cell is a miniature chemical factory that produces the materials and energy that the body needs. Among the specialized cells in your body are nerve cells, blood cells, muscle cells, skin cells, and reproductive cells. Although cells can vary in size, they are usually very small. Some are microscopic, while others are the size of a speck of dust. Cells also vary in shape according to their function in the body. Muscle cells are long and smooth; skin cells are rectangular in shape; red blood cells are round and flat. Long, thin nerve cells branch out like trees throughout the body (see illustration: Types of Cells).

The Makeup of Cells   Cell structure can vary among different kinds of cells. Most cells, however, consist of three major parts: the membrane, the nucleus, and the cytoplasm (see illustration: Major Parts of a Composite Cell). The *membrane* is a layer of fat and protein that surrounds the cell and helps maintain the cell's shape. Nutrients are able to enter the cell through the membrane, and waste products leave the cell the same way.

The *nucleus* is the information storage area and control center of the cell. It contains threadlike bodies called *chromosomes*. Each chromosome has a string of *genes* made up of DNA (deoxyribonucleic acid). DNA contains the instructions for producing the proteins and ENZYMES that the cell needs to function. Genes also carry the genetic information that determines a person's physical characteristics. One gene, for example, dictates the color of a person's hair or eyes; another may control height or skin color.

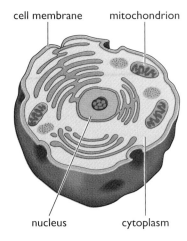

cell membrane   mitochondrion

nucleus   cytoplasm

Major Parts of a Composite Cell. *Although body cells vary in size, shape, and structure, they all have the same basic components. The cell shown here is a generalized view that includes the most important parts of all cells.*

The *cytoplasm*, which consists of fluid and a network of tubing, fills the rest of the area within the cell membrane. Most of the cell's chemical reactions occur in the cytoplasm in tiny structures called *organelles*. The organelles are suspended in the cytoplasm and perform specific functions. Among the most important of these organelles are the *mitochondria* (sing. *mitochondrion*), which oxidize or burn nutrients to produce energy for the cell.

Cell Reproduction   Cells reproduce by dividing in one of two ways: mitosis or meiosis. In *mitosis*, each cell splits in half and forms two identical "daughter cells." Then each of the daughter cells splits into four cells, and each of those cells splits into eight cells, and so on. When mitosis occurs, the chromosomes also split into pairs so that each new cell receives an identical set of chromosomes.

Reproductive cells, however, divide by *meiosis*. Instead of duplicating themselves, reproductive cells produce egg and sperm cells with only half as many chromosomes. In humans, normal cells have 46 chromosomes, but when the reproductive cells divide, each cell is left with only 23 chromosomes. When two people conceive a child, their reproductive cells come together and their chromosomes recombine into the normal number of 46, which is how children inherit characteristics from both parents. The study of such inheritable characteristics is called genetics.

Disorders of the Cells   Sometimes when meiosis occurs, chromosomes may be lost, a chromosome may be left behind, or too many chromosomes may be passed on. When this happens, a child may be born with a genetic or congenital defect or disease. One of the most common genetic disorders is Down syndrome. In Down syndrome, the child inherits an extra chromosome, which results in mental retardation and abnormal physical characteristics. Other genetic disorders include sickle cell anemia, cystic fibrosis, cleft palate, heart defects, webbed fingers or toes, and color blindness. Many of these disorders, such as cleft palate and certain heart defects, can be corrected surgically. In other disorders, such as Down syndrome and cystic fibrosis, certain symptoms can be relieved, but the underlying cause cannot be treated. (See also TISSUE; GENETICS, **6**.)

▶ CHEST

The chest, or thorax, is the upper part of the trunk of the body. It extends from the base of the neck to the DIAPHRAGM (MUSCLE), which is a sheet of muscle between the chest and the abdomen. The bony structure of the chest provides protection for the HEART, LUNGS, and major blood vessels within the chest.

The chest skeleton includes the *rib cage* and the *sternum*. The rib cage is made up of 12 pairs of ribs. All the ribs are connected to the spine at the back. The upper 10 pairs are also attached either directly or indirectly to the sternum at the front. The lower 2 pairs, the floating ribs, are attached only to the spine. The *intercostal muscles* connect the ribs and enable you to expand and contract your chest during breathing (see illustration: The Chest).

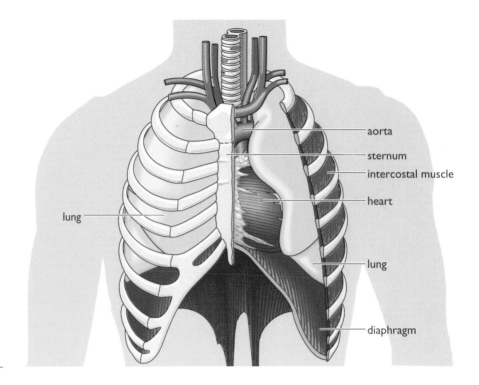

aorta

sternum

intercostal muscle

heart

lung

lung

diaphragm

The Chest.

The sternum is the long, flat, narrow bone in the middle of your chest. It has three parts: the manubrium (mah NU bree um), the body, and the xiphoid (ZIF oid) process. A joint between the manubrium and the body allows these parts to move independently during breathing.

CONSULT A PHYSICIAN

The ribs provide a protective framework, but they can break. Broken ribs from falls, accidents, or sporting injuries need to be checked by a physician. The danger is that a sharp bone fragment could pierce one of the vital organs within the chest cavity. The ribs may also be a site for tumors, both benign and malignant.

► **CHILD DEVELOPMENT** Infant and child development occurs in fairly predictable stages marked by the mastery of developmental skills. Most children reach these stages in physical, social, emotional, and intellectual GROWTH at roughly the same age. However, some variation is perfectly normal.

Stages of Development *Infancy* is the period from birth to 18 months. Reflex actions, such as sucking and grasping, begin to disappear as voluntary actions, such as reaching and crawling, are mastered. In learning to control their body movements, most infants begin with the head and then work down through the arms, trunk, and legs. Raising the head, turning, sitting, crawling, and walking are all developmental skills of this stage.

The *toddler* stage extends from 18 months to 3 years of age. This is the time when speech, muscle coordination, and hand-eye coordination are fine-tuned. One- or two-word phrases are expanded into complete sentences. Simple toys and games, such as riding a tricycle and stringing spools, help the toddler control and develop large and small muscles. Toddlers have strong bonds with parents and care givers. By age 3, many

Child Development. *While there is some variation in the age at which children reach certain levels of physical, emotional, intellectual, and social development, nearly all children develop skills in the same order. For example, most infants learn to walk only after they have mastered sitting up, crawling, and standing.*

toddlers begin to develop the social skills they need to play with others. Toilet training to gain control of the bowels and bladder is another important developmental task at this stage.

The *preschool* stage covers ages 3 to 5. The preschooler desperately wants to be independent but still looks to adults for reassurance. At this stage the child learns and tests standards of behavior. Preschoolers have high energy levels. They question everything they see: "Why do fish swim?" Developmental skills include the ability to hop on one foot, copy a circle on paper, manage social situations with peers, and speak clearly.

The *early school* years extend from ages 5 through 8. This is a period of major development in social, emotional, and intellectual growth. Coping with school and a wider circle of friends may produce anxiety in some children. This usually disappears, however, with parental support and the help of a sensitive teacher. At this stage, children continue to develop their self-image and begin comparing themselves to others. Their problem-solving abilities improve, and they begin to make choices.

The *preadolescent*, or preteen, stage extends from about age 8 to age 12 or 13. Physical growth increases dramatically and includes the development of sexual characteristics. The child at this stage shows an increased dependence on friends as opposed to family.

Factors That Affect Child Development Infants inherit from their parents a variety of genetic "codes" that will affect their size, shape, intelligence, and other aspects of their development. The type of environment they grow up in also influences their development in significant ways. Experts disagree on the relative importance of heredity versus environment on a child's development. (See also ADOLESCENCE.)

▶ **CIRCULATORY SYSTEM** The circulatory system, also referred to as the *cardiovascular system*, consists of the HEART and blood vessels. A vast network of VEINS, ARTERIES, and even smaller vessels called CAPILLARIES carries blood to every part of the body so that it can perform its vital functions.

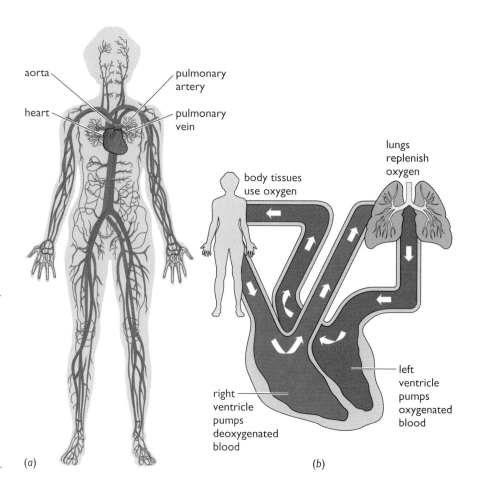

aorta

pulmonary
artery

heart

pulmonary
vein

lungs
replenish
oxygen

body tissues
use oxygen

left
ventricle
pumps
oxygenated
blood

right
ventricle
pumps
deoxygenated
blood

(a)

(b)

Circulatory System.

Illustration (a) depicts the body's network of veins and arteries. Illustration (b) is a simplified view of the circulatory system. Blood travels from the heart's left ventricle through the aorta into arteries throughout the body. After giving up oxygen and nutrients and absorbing waste products, the blood travels via the veins to the heart's right side. From here the pulmonary artery carries the blood to the lungs, where its oxygen is replenished. Then the blood travels through the pulmonary vein to the left side of the heart, where the process begins again.

This network delivers *oxygen* and nutrients to the CELLS and takes away waste products such as *carbon dioxide*.

How Circulation Works The circulatory system has two major loops (see illustration: Circulatory System). The first is the *systemic circulation*. Blood cells traveling through this loop are initially pumped out of the left side (left ventricle) of the heart into the AORTA, the body's main artery. The aorta soon branches into smaller arteries and then into *arterioles,* which are smaller still. These empty into the tiny *capillaries* that lace every part of the body. Capillaries have walls so thin that oxygen, nutrients, and water easily pass through them into the surrounding tissue. At the same time, carbon dioxide and other waste products are absorbed back into the bloodstream. The blood then returns through a network of veins to the right side (right atrium) of the heart.

Next, blood passes from the right atrium to the right ventricle, beginning the circulatory system's second loop, *pulmonary circulation*. The heart's right ventricle pumps the blood through the pulmonary artery to the lungs. There, the carbon dioxide leaves the bloodstream and is replaced by oxygen, and the blood returns through the pulmonary veins to the left side of the heart, to begin the first loop again.

With every heartbeat, blood surges through the arteries—you can feel it when you take your pulse. Blood is under less pressure in the veins, where it flows more slowly and smoothly. Many veins have one-way *valves* to prevent the blood from reversing direction.

Common Circulatory Problems Bruises and swelling occur when a blow ruptures capillaries and blood leaks out into the surrounding tissue. More serious problems include *hypertension* (high blood pressure), which occurs when the pressure rises too high in the arteries. In *atherosclerosis*, a material called *plaque* builds up inside the arteries, narrowing them and restricting or blocking the blood flow. When it affects the coronary arteries, which serve the heart, atherosclerosis can cause a *heart attack*. If atherosclerosis occurs in the brain, it can cause a *stroke*.

HEALTHY CHOICES
●●●●●●●●●●●●

How to Prevent Problems Hypertension runs in families. If it runs in yours, you may be able to prevent this condition by limiting your sodium and salt intake and keeping your weight down. You are less likely to develop atherosclerosis if you eat foods low in saturated fat and cholesterol and do not smoke. Aerobic exercise also helps keep the circulatory system healthy. (See also ATHEROSCLEROSIS, 3; CARDIOVASCULAR DISEASE, 3; HYPERTENSION, 3; VARICOSE VEIN, 3; AEROBIC EXERCISE, 4.)

► **COLON** see DIGESTIVE SYSTEM

► **CONNECTIVE TISSUE** Connective tissues are specialized fibers that bind together and support the tissues and structures of the body. Together with the muscles and bones, connective tissues make it possible for you to move.

Cartilage, ligaments, and tendons are the major connective tissues. Other connective tissues include various fibrous membranes and the loose webs of fibers that run through the body's tissues.

Cartilage Cartilage is a strong, extremely dense form of connective tissue. It is made up mostly of a gel-like substance called *collagen*. Cartilage plays an important role in the skeletal system, acting as a cushion in your joints. There are three main types of cartilage.

> ► The first type, hyaline cartilage, lines joint surfaces such as the knee, reducing friction and easing motion in the joint. It is smooth and tough.
> ► The second type, fibrocartilage, is found in the disks between the bones of the spine and in pads of tissue that cushion joints. Fibrocartilage contains large amounts of collagen and is very strong.
> ► The third type, elastic cartilage, is found in the outer part of the ear and is soft and rubbery.

Ligaments Ligaments are important components of the joints, connecting the bones at the joint. Ligaments form bands of slightly elastic, fibrous, white tissue. These tough bands prevent the bones from moving too much or separating. In addition, ligaments support various internal organs such as the bladder and liver and a woman's breasts.

Tendons   Tendons connect muscle to bone and muscle to muscle. The collagen in tendons makes them very strong and flexible. Most tendons are cylindrical. In a few areas, however, such as the abdominal wall muscles, the tendons form wide fibrous sheets. Some tendons, including those in the hands, wrists, and feet, are surrounded by fibers called *synovial sheaths*. The sheaths secrete synovial fluid, which lubricates the tendons and lessens friction. You can see the tendons that attach your forearm muscles to your finger muscles at work when you drum your fingers on the table.

Common Problems of Connective Tissues   Connective tissue loses its elasticity as your body ages. Collagen molecules tend to clump together, making the tissue more rigid and less flexible. Elastic connective tissue loses its ability to snap back.

A variety of disorders and injuries also affect connective tissues. Tissues can be torn or damaged by the vigorous jumping and twisting in basketball, for example. Injuries can lead to complications such as inflammation of a tendon (*tendinitis*). Finally, some illnesses (for example, rheumatoid arthritis) can injure connective tissue. Treatments for connective tissue disorders include application of ice, bandaging, elevation of the limb, physical or ultrasound therapy, anti-inflammatory and other drugs, immobilization, and surgery. (See also ARTHRITIS, **3**; TENDINITIS, **3**; SPORTS INJURIES, **4**.)

► DEATH

Death is the end of life, the irreversible termination of all biological function. Normally, physicians diagnose *biological death* when a person's lungs and heart stop functioning and when the pupils of the eyes remain dilated and unresponsive to light. Millions of people have experienced a condition known as *clinical death*, when their hearts and lungs stopped temporarily until they were revived by physicians or rescue workers. The cells of the body start to deteriorate within minutes of clinical death.

In recent years, modern technological advances have made it possible for machines to continue lung and heart function in an otherwise dead body. These advances created the need for another definition of death, and in 1968, the Harvard Medical School developed the concept of *brain death*. According to this definition, a person is dead if the entire brain has irreversibly ceased to function. The Harvard guidelines state that physicians must determine that the person does not respond to any stimuli, that there are no reflexes, that the person cannot breathe independently, and that there is no electrical activity in the brain.

Sometimes death comes suddenly; for example, as a result of physical injury or heart attack. For most people, however, dying is a gradual process that enables the dying person and his or her family and friends to come to terms with it. People who are dying need to be able to talk to their loved ones about their feelings of anger, guilt, fear, and regret. More and more people are now choosing to die at home or in *hospices*, special units in a hospital or separate facilities for the dying, where they can be relieved of pain, maintain their dignity, and die in a calm and reassuring setting. (See also DYING AND BEREAVEMENT, **5**; HOSPICE, **9**.)

> For most people, dying is a gradual process that enables the dying person and his or her family and friends to come to terms with it.

▶ DENTAL EXAMINATION

A dental examination is an examination of the condition of a person's mouth, teeth, gums, and the bone that holds the teeth in place. The exam typically includes taking a medical history, examining the mouth, and cleaning the teeth. The purpose is usually a routine checkup or an examination to diagnose and treat a specific problem.

The Medical History   The dentist or *dental hygienist* asks about a person's general health to learn about any physical conditions that may be affected by dental treatment. For instance, people with diabetes, certain heart conditions, and allergies may need special dental treatment. The dentist usually makes a note of medications that the person takes to avoid prescribing any drugs that could cause harmful interactions.

The Examination   The actual examination involves a thorough assessment of the mouth. The dentist examines the gums and soft tissues of the mouth to look for redness, puffiness, or bleeding that may indicate *gingivitis* (gum inflammation) or *periodontitis* (a disease of the gum and bone that support the teeth). The patient's bite and teeth are examined as a whole to evaluate points of contact between the teeth and to check for excessive movement in individual teeth during chewing.

Next, the dentist uses a probe and small mirror to examine teeth individually for signs of decay, looking specifically for cracks in the tooth enamel, discolored areas, and signs of new cavities. The dentist also uses the probe to check for periodontal disease around the base of the teeth.

When a cavity is suspected, the dentist will probably want to X-ray the area to detect decay hidden between the teeth or under the gum line and to diagnose the extent of decay. X rays also help evaluate bone damage from periodontal disease; find fractures, abscesses, and tumors; and check the condition of impacted wisdom teeth (molars that have not broken through the gums). When X rays are taken, the body is protected by a lead apron even though radiation dosage in dental diagnosis is extremely small.

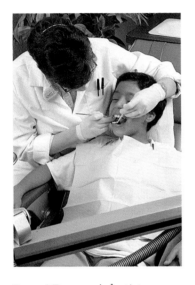

Dental Exam. *A dentist uses a tool called a probe to detect signs of tooth decay: cracks in the enamel, discolored areas, or cavities.*

The Cleaning Process   Cleaning the teeth, a process called *prophylaxis*, helps maintain the health of teeth and gums. This procedure may be performed by either the dentist or the dental hygienist. Cleaning removes *calculus* (also called tartar), which is *plaque* (a sticky substance) that has hardened and stuck to the teeth. Calculus is removed with a sharp instrument called a scaler or by a vibrating ultrasonic device. The teeth are then polished with special toothpaste applied by a tool with rotating rubber heads. This helps smooth the teeth so that plaque will be less likely to stick to their surfaces. Children and teenagers may receive a fluoride application to prevent tooth decay. Before or during the cleaning, patients are often instructed in brushing and flossing techniques.

Dental Examinations and Oral Health   Dental checkups and cleanings are usually recommended twice a year, although frequency should be determined on an individual basis. People who get many cavities, take poor care of their teeth, or drink and smoke excessively may need to see a dentist more often. Adults who have no decay and take good care of their teeth and gums may need a checkup and cleaning only once a year. (See also TOOTH; DENTAL PROBLEMS, 3; GUM DISEASE, 3; DENTAL CARE, 9.)

 RISK FACTORS
▶ ▶ ▶ ▶ ▶ ▶

▶ **DIAPHRAGM (MUSCLE)** The diaphragm is a dome-shaped sheet of muscle that separates the chest from the abdomen. It is attached to the spine, lower ribs, and sternum. The diaphragm is part of the RESPIRATORY SYSTEM.

How the Diaphragm Works When you inhale, the diaphragm muscle contracts and moves downward toward the abdomen. At the same time, the muscles between the ribs contract, pushing the ribs upward and outward. These actions enlarge the chest cavity. This gives the lungs room to expand and fill with air (see illustration: How the Diaphragm Works).

How the Diaphragm Works.
When you inhale, your diaphragm flattens and your rib cage expands. This makes room for the air you have breathed in. When you exhale, the opposite happens. Your diaphragm relaxes and rib cage contracts, squeezing out the air from your lungs.

When you exhale, the diaphragm muscle relaxes, returning to its original position. As a result, the chest cavity becomes smaller and gently compresses the lungs to force the air, now depleted of oxygen, back up and out through your mouth and nose.

While at rest, you breathe 13 to 17 times per minute. During exercise, however, muscles need more oxygen, so you may take up to 80 breaths a minute.

Common Problems *Hiccups* are spasms of the diaphragm muscle. As the diaphragm contracts spasmodically, air is breathed in. At the same time, the glottis (the structure that surrounds the vocal cords) closes suddenly and produces the hiccup sound. Usually, the diaphragm will return to its normal contract/relax pattern and the hiccups will go away on their own. (See also LUNG; HICCUPS, **3**.)

▶ **DIGESTIVE SYSTEM** The digestive system consists of a long tube called the *alimentary canal,* or digestive canal, that extends from the mouth through the stomach to the large intestine. It also includes several related organs: the SALIVARY GLANDS, the LIVER, the GALLBLADDER, and the PANCREAS. Each part plays a specific role in the digestive system's job of breaking food down into simpler substances that your body can use for energy and growth.

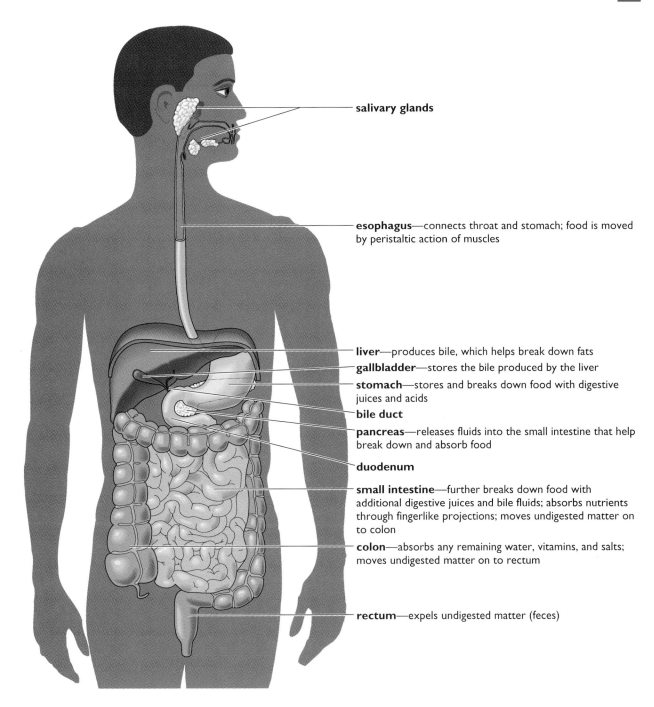

salivary glands

esophagus—connects throat and stomach; food is moved by peristaltic action of muscles

liver—produces bile, which helps break down fats

gallbladder—stores the bile produced by the liver

stomach—stores and breaks down food with digestive juices and acids

bile duct

pancreas—releases fluids into the small intestine that help break down and absorb food

duodenum

small intestine—further breaks down food with additional digestive juices and bile fluids; absorbs nutrients through fingerlike projections; moves undigested matter on to colon

colon—absorbs any remaining water, vitamins, and salts; moves undigested matter on to rectum

rectum—expels undigested matter (feces)

Digestive System.

Structure of the Digestive System   The alimentary canal begins in the MOUTH and continues as a long, smooth tube in the THROAT (pharynx) and the *esophagus,* a muscular section linking the throat and stomach (see illustration: Digestive System). The *stomach* is a hollow organ designed to expand when filled with food; it can, in fact, hold as much as 3 pints (about 1.5 L) of food. Special cells lining the stomach secrete *digestive enzymes* (substances that trigger chemical reactions) and stomach acids. However, the stomach and other digestive organs are also lined with mucus, which protects them from these powerful acids. Valves connect the throat to the esophagus, the esophagus to the stomach, and the stomach to the upper part of the small intestine. The *small intestine*, a 20-foot-long (6-meter-long) muscular tube bundled in the abdomen, has three sections: the *duodenum*, the *ileum*, and the *jejunum*. The inner walls of the small intestine have many small fingerlike projections filled with blood vessels. The intestinal walls also contain glands that produce additional digestive enzymes. Ducts connect the small intestine to the pancreas, liver, and gallbladder. At its lower end, the small intestine connects to the large intestine, or colon. Much shorter and wider than the small intestine, the *colon* has a smooth inner lining. Its several sections wind around the abdomen and lead into the RECTUM.

> Digestion is both physical and chemical. Both processes begin in the mouth as food is cut and ground into small pieces by your teeth and lubricated by saliva.

How the Digestive System Works Digestion is both physical and chemical. Both processes begin in the mouth as food is cut and ground into small pieces by your teeth and lubricated by saliva. *Saliva*, a liquid produced by the salivary glands in your mouth, contains a digestive enzyme that begins to break starches down into simple sugars that give you energy. As you chew, your tongue forms small balls of food that can be swallowed easily. To prevent choking, a small flap called the *epiglottis* covers your airway when the throat valve opens to let food into the esophagus. Circular muscles in the esophagus contract in waves called *peristalsis* to push the food down toward the stomach. Peristalsis, not gravity, moves the food; valves at both ends of the esophagus keep food from flowing back up the alimentary canal.

Both physical and chemical digestion continue in the stomach. Muscles in the stomach walls stir food around, mixing it with the digestive juices and acids produced by the stomach lining. The juices further break down the carbohydrates, proteins, and fats in food, and the stomach's ability to store food allows you to go for several hours between meals without getting hungry.

The food, now almost liquid, passes from the stomach into the *duodenum*. Its presence there stimulates the release of bile and digestive juices by the liver, gallbladder, and pancreas. The *bile* helps the body digest fat, while the pancreatic enzymes mix with those secreted by the small intestine itself. As peristalsis pushes the liquid through the intestine, its chemical breakdown is completed. The digested substances are absorbed into the bloodstream and lymphatic system through the many vessels in the intestinal walls. The remaining liquid and undigested fiber (mostly from vegetables) flows into the colon. Here most of the water and any remaining vitamins or salts are reabsorbed into the bloodstream through the colon lining. All that remains is undigested matter and cells that the lining continually discards. These are expelled from the body as feces.

Common Digestive Problems *Ulcers*, or sores, may form in the stomach or duodenum if digestive acids destroy the protective mucus on their linings. If bile in the gallbladder contains too much cholesterol, *gallstones* may form. Gallstones that are lodged in a bile duct can be very painful and may have to be surgically removed. Other gastrointestinal disorders include infections in the digestive tract caused by bacteria, parasites, viruses, and even allergies. The digestive system is also very sensitive to a person's overall state of health and may react to general illness, tiredness, or stress with minor symptoms such as heartburn or diarrhea.

How to Avoid Problems You are less likely to develop a gastrointestinal disorder if you eat a balanced diet, exercise regularly, and get enough rest. You should try to keep stress to a manageable level and avoid excessive alcohol intake, which can damage the liver. Be sure to wash your hands before preparing and eating food. Poultry and meat should be thoroughly cooked, and fruits and vegetables well washed. Research also indicates that a diet high in fiber and low in fat may prevent certain kinds of intestinal cancer. (See also DIARRHEA, **2**; GALLSTONES, **3**; STOMACHACHE/INDIGESTION, **3**; ULCER, PEPTIC, **3**; DIETARY GUIDELINES, **4**.)

▶ EAR

The ear performs two major functions: hearing and balance. It is an intricate organ composed of three sections: the outer ear, the middle ear, and the inner ear (see illustration: How the Ear Works).

Outer Ear The outer ear, the part of the ear that projects from the side of the head, is made up of the *pinna*, or auricle, and the outer ear canal. The pinna consists of folds of cartilage and skin that are shaped like a funnel to collect sound waves. The sound waves or vibrations travel through the outer ear canal to the middle ear. The canal is lined with hair follicles and skin glands that secrete earwax to trap foreign objects and dust.

How the Ear Works. *After reaching the pinna, sound waves pass through the outer ear canal and cause the eardrum to vibrate. These vibrations are transmitted to the hammer, anvil, and stirrup of the middle ear and pass through the oval window to the inner ear. In the cochlea, the vibrations are changed into nerve impulses that travel along the auditory nerve to the brain. The brain interprets the sound. The vestibule and semicircular canals of the inner ear are responsible for balance.*

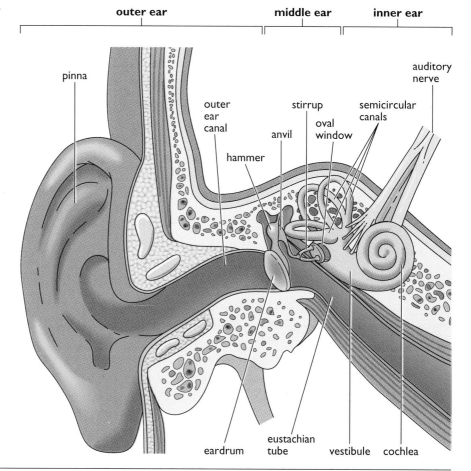

outer ear   middle ear   inner ear

pinna · outer ear canal · hammer · anvil · stirrup · oval window · semicircular canals · auditory nerve · eardrum · eustachian tube · vestibule · cochlea

> The eardrum transmits the sound waves or vibrations from the outer ear to three tiny bones that intensify the vibrations and pass them on to the inner ear.

Middle Ear   The outer ear is separated from the middle ear by a thin circular membrane called the tympanic membrane, or *eardrum.* The eardrum transmits the sound waves or vibrations from the outer ear to three tiny bones that intensify the vibrations and pass them on to the inner ear. The bones—the *hammer* (malleus), *anvil* (incus), and *stirrup* (stapes)—are named for their shapes. The base of the stirrup bone is attached to the *oval window,* a membrane that leads to the inner ear. A narrow canal called the *eustachian tube* connects the middle ear to the throat. The eustachian tube's function is to equalize the air pressure of the middle ear and of the air outside. Muscles open this tube whenever you swallow or yawn.

Inner Ear   The inner ear, or *labyrinth,* is an intricate, fluid-filled structure consisting of the cochlea, the vestibule, and the semicircular canals. The *cochlea,* the part of the inner ear concerned with hearing, looks like a snail shell. This coiled tube is filled with tiny hairs that are stimulated by sound waves. The hairs transmit sound vibrations to the *auditory nerve,* which carries them to the brain. There the vibrations are interpreted as specific sounds. The *vestibule* connects the cochlea to the semicircular canals. The vestibule plays a role, along with the semicircular canals, in your sense of motion and balance. Set at right angles to each other, the three semicircular canals are filled with fluid that reacts to changes of motion or position. The canals also send information to the brain via the auditory nerve so that it can maintain the body's balance.

Ear Problems   *Earaches* are caused by a wide variety of ailments, including colds, sinus infections, and water trapped in the ear. Hearing loss or deafness is sometimes caused by hereditary abnormalities in the ear. Hearing loss may also be the result of a blow that damages the auditory nerve, of repeated exposure to loud noise, of disease, or of deterioration of the inner ear.

CONSULT A
PHYSICIAN

HEALTHY CHOICES
●●●●●●●●●●●●●

Ear Care   If you experience painful or persistent earaches, consult a physician. Clean the outer portion of the ear daily with a soft washcloth or cotton swab. Never use a cotton swab or any other object to clean wax out of the ear canal. Wear earplugs when swimming and diving and when working around loud machinery. Finally, do not listen to loud music through headsets. (See also EAR INFECTIONS, **2**; HEARING LOSS, **3**.)

▶ **ELBOW**

The elbow is the JOINT that connects the bone of the upper arm to the bones of the forearm. This *hinge joint* allows the arm to bend and straighten. In addition, smaller joints within the elbow allow the forearm to rotate from side to side. Together with the shoulder joint, the elbow enables the arm to make a wide range of motions.

The elbow joint is made up of three bones: the *humerus* in the upper arm and the *ulna* and *radius* in the forearm (see illustration: The Elbow). *Ligaments* connect these bones and prevent movement that is beyond the range of the joint. The muscles of the upper arm, the *triceps* and *biceps,* control the movement of the elbow. *Tendons* from these muscles extend across the elbow and connect with the forearm bones. When the biceps contracts, the tendons pull the forearm bones forward and the arm bends. When the triceps contracts, the tendons pull the forearm back and the arm straightens. A layer of smooth *cartilage* covers the ends of the bones, allowing them to slide over one another at the elbow. In addition, the *synovial membrane*, which surrounds the elbow joint, secretes a fluid that cushions and lubricates these bones. The olecranon, or "funny bone," is the bony tip of the ulna at the rear of the elbow.

Common Elbow Problems   The elbow is vulnerable to sports injuries. In fact, some of the most common elbow injuries are named after particular sports. *Tennis elbow* and *golfer's elbow,* for example, refer to strained tendons or ligaments. But you do not need to play sports to suffer elbow injuries; sudden, violent twists or repetitive motions can strain and injure the elbow. In addition, falls or sharp blows can lead to fractures or dislocations. These require a physician's attention. Elbow joints are also susceptible to degenerative diseases, such as osteoarthritis, in which the cartilage and bones wear away, causing pain and loss of mobility.

To prevent injury to the elbows, you should wear elbow pads when playing vigorous sports. If you do injure your elbow, rest it by avoiding the same sharp or repetitive motions that may have caused the injury. (See also CONNECTIVE TISSUE; MUSCULOSKELETAL SYSTEM; TENDINITIS, 3.)

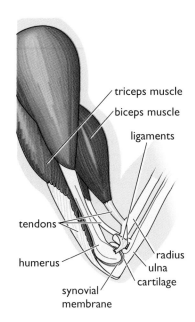

triceps muscle
biceps muscle
ligaments
tendons
humerus
radius
ulna
cartilage
synovial membrane

The Elbow.

▶ ENDOCRINE SYSTEM

The endocrine system is a group of glands that work together to control body processes. Each GLAND produces a different type of chemical messenger, or HORMONE, and releases it into the bloodstream to influence specific *target tissues* or *target organs.* A healthy endocrine system efficiently coordinates normal body processes and enables the body to respond quickly to stress and other stimuli.

The glands that make up the endocrine system are located throughout the body and include the pituitary, the thyroid and parathyroid glands, the pancreas, the adrenal glands, the ovaries, and the testes (see illustration: Glands of the Endocrine System). These glands influence virtually every system of the body and are responsible for a range of activities, from controlling growth and reproduction, to maintaining body fluid levels, to responding to stressful situations. The endocrine glands have no tubes or ducts and release hormones directly into the bloodstream.

How the Endocrine System Works   Although each endocrine gland releases hormones independently, hormone levels in the blood are centrally monitored and controlled by a part of the brain called the HYPOTHALAMUS. At any moment 30 to 40 different hormones are present in the blood. When the hypothalamus detects too much or too little of a specific hormone, it signals the PITUITARY GLAND, which in turn signals the gland responsible for over- or underproducing the hormone. The pituitary is called the master gland because of its function in producing trophic (gland-stimulating) hormones that control other endocrine glands. In addition, some endocrine hormones are released in response to nerve impulses from the NERVOUS SYSTEM. For example, as part of the

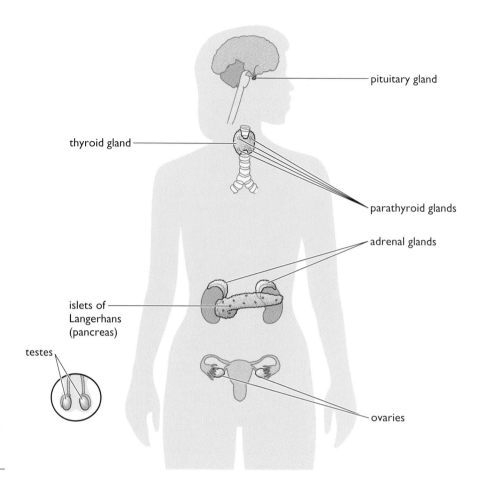

pituitary gland

thyroid gland

parathyroid glands

adrenal glands

islets of
Langerhans
(pancreas)

testes

ovaries

Glands of the Endocrine System. *The glands of the endocrine system release their hormones directly into the bloodstream.*

stress response, the brain signals the ADRENAL GLANDS to produce epinephrine, a hormone that makes the heart beat faster and produces a surge of energy.

The Role of Individual Endocrine Glands   In its role of stimulating other endocrine glands, the pituitary gland secretes a group of hormones. These include growth hormone (GH) to regulate the body's growth and thyroid-stimulating hormone to control production of hormones vital to body metabolism. The THYROID GLAND produces hormones that stimulate metabolism, body heat, and bone growth. The *parathyroid glands* maintain calcium level in the blood. Clusters of specialized cells in the PANCREAS called the *islets of Langerhans* secrete insulin and glucagon to help the body utilize glucose. The adrenal glands produce hormones that affect metabolism and maintain blood pressure and the salt level in the body. The *ovaries* produce estrogen and progesterone that control the development and function of female physiology, while the *testes* produce testosterone to stimulate male development and production of sperm.

Disorders of the Endocrine System   Endocrine-related disorders are the result of over- or underproduction of hormones. These disorders may result from a malfunction of the pituitary gland or hypothalamus that affects their role in controlling other glands. Disorders also may be due to a tumor or diseases affecting individual glands. Symptoms vary according to which gland is affected. For instance, *diabetes* occurs when the pancreas fails to produce insulin to regulate blood sugar levels. And thyroid gland problems can slow the growth and development of children and result in weight gain, hair loss, and goiter (swollen thyroid gland) in adults. Some endocrine gland disorders can be corrected by injections of the missing hormone.

Maintaining Endocrine System Health   Good diet and exercise habits help maintain a healthy endocrine system. Eat a well-balanced diet with enough calories and a proper amount of fat. Excessive exercise in hot weather with inadequate fluid intake can be harmful, so exercise moderately and drink plenty of liquids. Avoid the use of drugs that have not been prescribed and addictive substances such as alcohol and tobacco. (See also THYROID DISORDERS, **3**.)

▶ ENDORPHINS

Endorphins are naturally occurring chemicals formed within the body that relieve pain. These powerful substances are similar in structure to morphine, a pain-relieving drug, but they have a much stronger effect.

Produced primarily by the PITUITARY GLAND, endorphins act at certain sites, called *opiate receptors*, that are located in the brain, spinal cord, and nerve endings. The opiate receptors govern pain sensations. Endorphins act at these sites to suppress the transmission of pain signals. Endorphins are also thought to play a role in controlling the body's response to stress, determining mood, and regulating the contractions of the intestinal wall. In addition, endorphins may be involved in regulating the release of growth hormones from the pituitary gland.

Evidence suggests that aerobic exercise stimulates the release of endorphins. This may explain why some people experience a mild euphoria after strenuous exercise. The release of endorphins also seems to be stimulated by acupuncture, an ancient Chinese method of relieving pain. Acupuncture involves the insertion of needles in the body at strategic points, stimulating nerves deep within the muscles. The pituitary gland responds by releasing endorphins. Acupuncture has been used successfully to anesthetize patients for surgery and to treat smoking, drug abuse, compulsive eating, and other addictive problems. (See also PAIN, **3**.)

▶ ENZYME

An enzyme is a substance that brings about and accelerates chemical reactions in the body by building up or breaking down compounds. Enzymes play a role in many body processes, ranging from food digestion to muscle contraction. But because they are *catalysts*, agents of change that remain unchanged, enzymes are not affected by the reactions they set off.

Enzymes are produced in the body's cells. They are *proteins*, very complex compounds made up of amino acids. Each cell makes the enzymes that are necessary to accomplish its job in the body. Each of the enzymes produced regulates only specific chemical reactions, because only those compounds necessary to the reaction will fit the enzyme (see

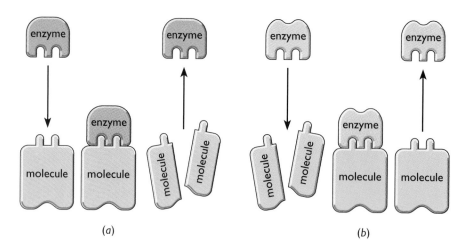

How Enzymes Work. (a) *An enzyme combines with a molecule, dividing it, then breaks away unchanged.* (b) *An enzyme combines with two molecules, building a larger molecule, then breaks away unchanged.*

(a)　　　　　　　(b)

illustration: How Enzymes Work). An enzyme might combine with a molecule and cause it to break down into smaller parts or might join two molecules to build a larger compound.

Problems with Enzymes Enzyme function can be affected by many factors, and the conditions must be just right for the enzyme to do its job. Temperature extremes, acids, and many salts will destroy the structure of enzymes. Certain drugs can also keep an enzyme from working properly by either increasing or blocking its action. Many enzymes need the addition of a component called a *coenzyme,* often a vitamin or a mineral, to achieve the chemical reaction.

Sometimes, a person will be born without certain enzymes. This condition is usually caused by an error in the genetic information inherited from parents and ancestors. Diseases such as cystic fibrosis are associated with the absence of certain enzymes.

Enzymes are useful in treating some diseases. For example, people who produce too much phlegm (FLEM) in their lungs can take enzymes that help loosen the phlegm so that they can expel it. Because many coenzymes come from vitamins or minerals, a balanced diet will help keep your enzymes working properly. (See also CYSTIC FIBROSIS, **3.**)

HEALTHY CHOICES
●●●●●●●●●●●●

EPINEPHRINE

Epinephrine (also called adrenaline) is a hormone secreted by the ADRENAL GLANDS. Under normal conditions, these glands release small quantities of epinephrine into the bloodstream. When the body is threatened, however, they suddenly release a large amount of the hormone all at once. Epinephrine is sometimes called the "emergency hormone" because its primary function is to prepare the body to deal with danger or stress.

The release of a large amount of epinephrine causes several changes in the body. The heart beats faster and the passageways in the lungs expand. Epinephrine also causes the blood vessels of the skin and digestive system to narrow, increasing the blood supply to the muscles. These changes, known as the fight-or-flight response, enable the body to react more quickly and powerfully to the immediate danger or threat it faces. If you have ever been frightened or experienced a near accident, you have probably felt the rapid heartbeat and other physical effects caused by the sudden release of a large amount of epinephrine.

RISK FACTORS
▶ ▶ ▶ ▶ ▶ ▶

Constant tension, stress, worry, or strong emotions such as fear or anger can stimulate the adrenal glands to produce too much epinephrine too frequently. This may result in elevated blood pressure and stress on the heart. Physicians recommend that people who suffer from excessive stress should exercise, learn relaxation techniques, and seek help in dealing with crises in their lives.

Adrenalin (with a capital *A* and no *e* at the end) is the trade name for epinephrine that is produced synthetically or taken from the glands of animals. Physicians use Adrenalin to stimulate the heart during cardiac arrest, to help control bleeding, and to treat severe asthma attacks. (See also HORMONE; STRESS, 5; STRESS-MANAGEMENT TECHNIQUES, 5.)

▷ **EXCRETORY SYSTEM**   The excretory system consists of the kidneys, liver, large intestine, lungs, and sweat glands. These organs and glands work in various ways to perform the vital function of keeping the body healthy by discharging waste material from it.

The KIDNEYS filter water and dissolved waste from the body in the form of urine. The LIVER and large intestine remove solid waste from food digestion and other body processes. The large intestine expels these wastes as feces. In the breathing process, the LUNGS release the carbon dioxide waste into the outside air. Finally, *sweat glands* in the skin rid the body of water and salt through perspiration in order to help maintain correct body temperature.

HEALTHY CHOICES
● ● ● ● ● ● ● ● ● ● ●

You can keep your excretory system healthy by eating a balanced diet and consuming plenty of liquids, especially water. Your lungs will remain healthiest if you exercise regularly and do not smoke. (See also DIGESTIVE SYSTEM; RESPIRATORY SYSTEM; URINARY TRACT; PERSPIRATION, 4.)

▷ **EYE**   The eyes are the organs of sight in humans. Light reflected from outside objects enters the eyes and creates an image of these objects on a layer of light-sensitive tissue at the back of the eyes. This image is converted into nerve impulses and sent to the brain for processing.

Structure of the Eye   The eye is a movable sphere held within a socket that is attached to the skull by six muscles, which allow you to move your eyes. The eye's outermost layer consists of the *cornea,* the transparent area on the front of the eye, and the *sclera,* a tough white coating (see illustration: Parts of the Eye). Behind the cornea is the *iris,* the colored portion of the eye surrounding the circular gap called the *pupil;* behind the iris is a flexible *lens.* As light passes through the

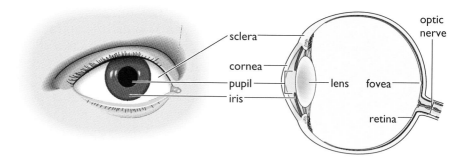

Parts of the Eye.

cornea and lens it is refracted, or bent. Muscles attached to the lens allow it to change shape so that objects at varying distance can be brought into focus (see illustration: How the Eye Focuses).

The interior of the eyeball, filled with a clear, jellylike fluid, is lined with a layer of nerve tissue called the *retina*. The retina contains two types of cells known by their shape as rods and cones. The *rods* are sensitive to varying degrees of light, including very dim light. They also provide peripheral vision, your view of areas to the side that you do not see very clearly. The *cones*, which are sensitive only to very bright light, enable you to distinguish between different colors. The rays of light refracted by the cornea and lens come together on the retina to form an image. The *fovea*, a small spot on the retina made up mostly of cones, produces the sharpest vision. The retina creates electrical nerve impulses that are transmitted from the back of the eye through the *optic nerve* and into the brain, where these impulses are interpreted as what we "see."

A ring of bone, consisting of the eyebrow, the bridge of the nose, and the cheekbone, protects the delicate structures of the eye. Keeping the eye free of dust and other foreign matter are the upper and lower eyelids, tears produced by glands in and around the upper eyelid, and the eyelashes. The amount of light that enters the eye is controlled by the eyelids and also by the iris, which expands or contracts the pupil. The light-sensitive cells of the retina can be irritated and sometimes damaged by too much light.

How the Eye Focuses. *Muscles attached to the lens enable you to focus by changing its shape. When you view objects that are close, the lens is short and fat; when you view objects that are distant, the lens is long and thin. Light reflected from an object passes through the lens, which projects the image onto the retina.*

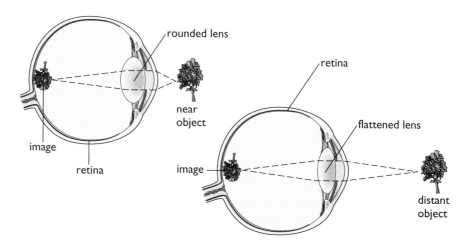

Eye Problems and Care   Even though the eyes have their own protective structures, they can still be damaged by injury and disease. To help prevent the sun from hurting your eyes, wear sunglasses in bright sunlight. Small objects that stray into your eyes may cause irritation and lead to infection. Wear safety goggles whenever there is particular danger, such as when riding a motorcycle or working with power tools. Eye makeup can cause irritation and allergic reactions. Never leave makeup on overnight; wash it off gently with warm water and mild soap.

Structural irregularities in the eye can cause vision problems. These can usually be corrected with prescription glasses or contact lenses or with surgery. In addition, parts of the eyes can develop various diseases that require medical attention. (See also CONJUNCTIVITIS, **2**; CATARACTS, **3**; EYE DISORDERS, **3**; GLAUCOMA, **3**; VISION PROBLEMS, **3**; EYE CARE, **9**.)

▶ FOOT

The foot is a complex structure of muscles, bones, and tendons that work together to cushion, balance, and propel the body. It is connected to the bones of the lower leg at the ankle joint.

The Structure of the Foot   The 26 bones of the foot are organized into three groups: the *tarsals*, the *metatarsals*, and the *phalanges* (see illustration: Bones of the Foot). (Note that the structure of the HAND, with 27 bones, is similar to the structure of the foot.) The tarsals are located toward the back of the foot and include the heel bone, or *calcaneus*, which is the largest bone in the foot.

The 5 metatarsals are the bones of the instep. The 14 phalanges are the toe bones. The phalanges are joined to the metatarsals at the ball of the foot. Each toe has 3 phalanges, except the big toe, which has 2. When you take a step, the big toe pushes off the ground, unbalancing the foot. The other toes act to bring the foot back in balance. The ANKLE joint connects the foot to the shinbones. The *Achilles tendon* runs down the back of the ankle and attaches the muscles of the calf to the heel bone.

Blood vessels, nerves, and tendons travel through and around the ankle joint to serve the foot. In addition, several strong ligaments hold

Bones of the Foot.   *The foot has 26 bones: 7 tarsals, 5 metatarsals, and 14 phalanges. The metatarsals, working with the heel bone, give the foot most of its leverage when you take a step.*

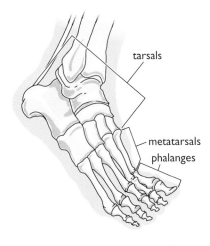

tarsals

metatarsals
phalanges

the bones of the feet together. The ligaments and muscles of the feet form two major arches, which act as shock absorbers to protect the spine from the jarring effects of walking and running. The bottom of the foot is covered by fat and a fibrous tissue. A thick, tough skin pads and protects the foot.

Disorders of the Foot   Because the foot must bear the entire weight of the body for many hours a day, it is subject to several ailments. Bunions, corns, and calluses (thickening and hardening of skin over the toe joints or on the bottom of the foot) are common. *Gout,* a form of arthritis, is an inflammation of the joint of the big toe or one of the other joints of the foot. *Athlete's foot,* a fungal disease, causes peeling and itching of the skin between the toes. Several over-the-counter preparations can be used to treat athlete's foot effectively. To avoid serious foot problems, you should always keep your feet clean and dry and wear comfortable shoes that fit well and support the arches of your feet. (See also ATHLETE'S FOOT, **2**; FOOT PROBLEMS, **3**; PODIATRIST, **9**.)

HEALTHY CHOICES

▶ GALLBLADDER

The gallbladder is an organ of the DIGESTIVE SYSTEM. Its main function is to store and concentrate *bile,* a liquid produced in the liver that helps in the digestion of fats.

Shaped like a pear, the gallbladder is connected to the LIVER by the bile duct and the smaller cystic duct (see illustration: Location of the Gallbladder). These ducts carry bile from the liver into the gallbladder. The lining of the gallbladder absorbs water from the bile, making it more concentrated, and the bile is then stored in the gallbladder. When food reaches the duodenum, hormones stimulate the gallbladder to contract and release bile. The bile travels through the cystic duct and the lower part of the bile duct and on into the small intestine.

Bile contains various salts and cholesterol. If the cholesterol in the bile becomes too concentrated, gallstones may form. When gallstones get stuck in one of the ducts, they can cause severe pain. Serious cases of

Location of the Gallbladder.

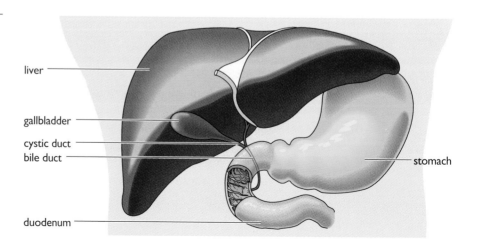

liver

gallbladder

cystic duct

bile duct

stomach

duodenum

gallstones are sometimes treated by removing the gallbladder. (See also GALLSTONES, **3**.)

▶ ## GLAND

Glands are groups of tissue that release chemical substances your body needs to function. Gland secretions help regulate growth and reproduction, aid in the digestion of food, adjust body temperature, monitor metabolism and blood pressure, lubricate body parts, maintain the balance of minerals and water in the cells, and prepare the body to deal with stress.

Some glands are single cells, but most are masses of cells. Glands are identified according to how they release their chemical substances. *Exocrine glands* secrete their substances onto a body surface or into a duct, or tube. Sweat glands, SALIVARY GLANDS, and tear glands are all exocrine glands.

Endocrine glands do not have ducts. They release their chemicals directly into the bloodstream, and the blood carries the substances to the places where they are needed. The chemicals released by the endocrine glands, called HORMONES, help regulate crucial body functions, including growth, reproduction, and digestion. Among the many endocrine glands are the PITUITARY GLAND, THYROID GLAND, and ADRENAL GLANDS.

Gland Disorders   Disorders of the glands can cause a wide variety of illnesses, including diabetes, caused by a lack of the digestive hormone insulin; *hypoglycemia,* or low blood sugar; and *hypothyroidism,* or underactivity of the thyroid gland. Most glandular disorders are treatable or controllable. (See also ENDOCRINE SYSTEM; METABOLISM; DIABETES, **3**; THYROID DISORDERS, **3**.)

▶ ## GROWTH

Growth is the progressive development that leads people from infancy through old age. It is a natural process that includes physical, intellectual, emotional, and social development. Good health and normal growth go hand in hand, and both are strongly influenced by a person's lifestyle.

Stages of Growth   For convenience, growth is often explained in terms of periods or stages that roughly approximate infancy, childhood, adolescence or puberty, young adulthood, middle age, older adulthood, and old age. Growth through these stages is cumulative; that is, the success of each stage is greatly influenced by the development that has taken place in the stages that have preceded it. The greatest growth occurs in infancy and early childhood, although puberty is another period of rapid growth (see graph: Average Physical Growth, Ages 1 to 14). For example, the healthy 5-year-old's brain has reached 90 percent of its adult size. If the brain's growth is slowed or otherwise affected by illness, malnutrition, or

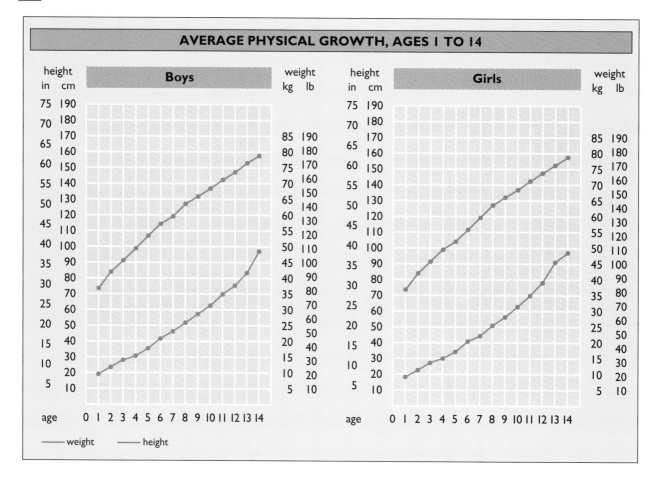

AVERAGE PHYSICAL GROWTH, AGES 1 TO 14

Boys

Girls

— weight   — height

abuse, a child may never realize his or her mental potential as an adult. During these same years, the healthy child learns trust, independence, and initiative.

Physical growth is an increase in size that takes place when the body produces new materials faster than the old ones are used up or worn out. Contributing to this increase in size are various HORMONES, chemicals that trigger changes in different structures of the body. Although significant physical growth ends at about the beginning of early adulthood, emotional, social, and intellectual growth may continue throughout life.

Factors That Affect Growth   A combination of heredity and environmental factors affect your growth. Your heredity is determined by the genes you inherit from your parents. Your environment includes everything that has had an influence on your life—including your family, your neighborhood, your schools, the foods you have eaten—from the time you were born. Your lifestyle can play an extremely important role in your growth. To help ensure healthy growth, it is important to maintain a nourishing and well-balanced diet; exercise regularly; avoid harmful substances such as alcohol, other drugs, and tobacco; and keep stress to a manageable level. It is also important to have regular medical checkups. Healthy habits established during early adulthood help ensure successful development throughout the rest of life. (See also ADOLESCENCE; ADULTHOOD; AGING; CHILD DEVELOPMENT; LIFESTYLE, 4.)

HEALTHY CHOICES
● ● ● ● ● ● ● ● ● ● ● ●

▶ Hair

Types of Hair. *The shape of the hair shaft determines whether your hair is curly or straight. The amount of melanin in the cortex determines the color of your hair.*

A hair is a thin, threadlike filament that projects from the skin. Almost all parts of the human body are covered with hair; the scalp alone may contain 100,000 hairs. Hair serves various functions. Hair on the head insulates the top of the skull, preventing heat loss through the scalp. Hair on the eyebrows and eyelids shields the eyes from light, and hair around the eyes, nose, and ears filters out dust and other foreign objects.

Hair Structure and Growth Hair grows in *follicles,* baglike structures embedded in the skin (see illustration: Hair Structure). When your hair is growing, the root of the follicle produces new hair cells that push old cells up and out. These old cells die and form the protein *keratin.* Eventually they are pushed through the outer layers of the skin as shafts of hair. Each hair shaft is composed of three layers: the medulla, the cortex, and the cuticle. The medulla, a semihollow core, is surrounded by long, thin fibers that make up the cortex. The amount of *melanin,* or dark pigment, in the cortex determines hair color. When the cortex loses all of its melanin, it becomes transparent and the hair turns white. The cuticle, the outermost layer of the hair, is a thin, colorless sheet. *Sebaceous glands* attached to each follicle produce oil to lubricate hair. The shape of your hair shaft determines whether it is straight or curly: Straight hairs are round; curly hairs are flat.

Each follicle alternates between periods of growth and periods of rest. When the follicle enters the rest period, the hair falls out. The root then starts to grow a new hair in the same follicle. Hair grows at a rate of about half an inch (about 1.3 cm) per month.

Hair Damage and Loss Split ends and brittle hair often result from excessive shampooing, bleaching, or brushing and occasionally from vitamin or mineral deficiencies.

Hair Structure.

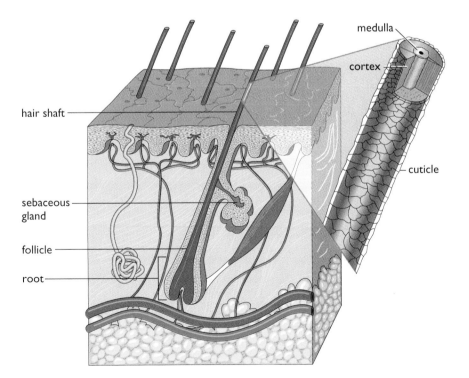

Normally, a person loses between 50 and 100 hairs a day. Baldness occurs when the roots fail to produce new hair at the end of the rest cycle. Male pattern baldness is an inherited trait in which the hairline recedes from the front and top of the scalp. Temporary hair loss can be caused by chemotherapy, some illnesses, and malnutrition. Harsh chemicals in hair dyes and permanent-wave solutions can also cause hair loss.

HEALTHY CHOICES

CONSULT A
PHYSICIAN

Hair Care   To reduce hair damage and loss, brush and comb your hair gently. Do not pull your hair or wear it in a tight braid or ponytail. Avoid too much sun, frequent permanents, use of hair dyes, bleaches, straightening solutions, and hot blow-drying. Use a mild shampoo and wash your hair regularly. Maintain a healthy diet, and see a doctor if you experience sudden, unexplained hair loss. (See also DANDRUFF, 3; HAIR LOSS, 3.)

► HAND

The hand is the most versatile and flexible part of the human body. It enables you to lift, grasp, and manipulate objects, and to perform movements as different as writing your name and throwing a ball. The hand's ability to perform so many tasks is due to the fact that the thumb and fingers move independently of each other, and the thumb can fold over and work with the fingers. Imagine trying to pick something up if you did not have a thumb.

> The hand is made up of 27 bones; 20 muscles; and a complex network of ligaments, tendons, nerves, and blood vessels.

The Structure of the Hand   The hand is made up of 27 bones; 20 muscles; and a complex network of ligaments, tendons, nerves, and blood vessels. The bones of the hand include the 8 *carpal* bones of the wrist; 5 long bones in the palm called *metacarpals*; and 14 finger bones, or *phalanges* (see illustration: Structure of the Hand).

The hand is capable of a wide range of motions. The elbow joint permits the hand to rotate (palm up or down), and the *wrist joint* allows the hand to bend backward and forward. Small *hinge joints* between each of the phalanges enable the fingers to bend and straighten. Strong *tendons* running down the front and back of each finger control these movements. The tendons connect muscles in the forearm and the palm with the bones in the fingers. Two major arteries supply blood to the hand.

The skin of the hand is very sensitive to touch and temperature. This heightened sensitivity helps the hand perform tasks that call for different degrees of pressure, from stroking a baby's delicate skin to wielding a hammer. The thin, horny plates on the tips of the fingers, the NAILS, protect the fingers and enable them to pick up small objects.

Common Hand Problems   We use our hands in nearly everything we do. This increases the possibility of burns, cuts, blisters, and fractures. The many small joints of the fingers, palms, and wrists are susceptible to arthritis, which causes pain, swelling, and in some cases, deformity. In recent years, *carpal tunnel syndrome* has become increasingly recognized among people who must perform repetitive hand movements, such as typing or cutting meat. In carpal tunnel syndrome, swollen tissues press on a major nerve that passes through the tunnel formed by the carpal

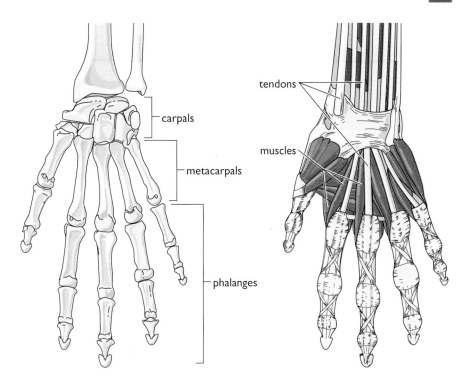

Structure of the Hand. *The 27 bones of the hand allow a wide variety of movements. These movements are made possible by tendons that attach the muscles of the forearm to the bones of the hand.*

carpals

metacarpals

phalanges

tendons

muscles

bones of the wrist, causing pain and weakness. The usual treatment for carpal tunnel syndrome is to rest the affected wrist and wear a brace while working. In some cases, surgery is required to create space for the nerve.

Many hand injuries can be prevented by wearing heavy gloves when working with tools and by being careful when handling sharp or dangerous objects. Gloves also protect the hands from skin irritations that can occur when the hands are exposed to harsh chemicals. (See also ARTHRITIS, **3**; CARPAL TUNNEL SYNDROME, **3**.)

HEALTHY CHOICES

▶ HEART

The heart is a remarkable organ composed of a special type of muscle that circulates thousands of gallons of BLOOD through your body every day. Located in the center of your chest and shaped more like a blunt-tipped cone than a valentine, the heart beats nonstop. Each time it beats it sends blood through the two loops of the CIRCULATORY SYSTEM. In the first loop, the heart pumps blood through all the blood vessels of your body. In the second loop, the heart sends the blood to the lungs to pick up oxygen.

Parts of the Heart The heart is made of a layer of muscle called the *myocardium* (from the Greek *myo*, meaning "muscle," and *kardia*, meaning "heart"). Lining the inside of this muscle is a thin, smooth membrane called the *endocardium*. Covering the outside is thin tissue called the *epicardium*. These layers are protected by a tough sac called the *pericardium*.

The heart is about the size of a clenched fist. It is divided by a vertical muscle wall called the *septum*, and each side forms a pump. The heart is further divided into four chambers, two on each side of the septum. The top two chambers are the left and right *atria* (sing. *atrium*); the bottom two chambers are the left and right *ventricles* (see illustration: The Heart).

How the Heart Works Your heart is designed to both send and receive the blood circulating throughout your body. During the active phase of the heart's cycle (*systole*), the different parts of the heart muscle contract, sending blood through the two circulatory routes in the body simultaneously (see illustration: The Heart Cycle). In the first loop, oxygenated blood from the lungs is pumped from the left atrium to the left ventricle and into the AORTA, the largest artery in the body. The aorta delivers the oxygen-rich blood for circulation to the tissues and organs of the body. In the second loop, deoxygenated blood that has traveled through the body is pumped from the right atrium to the right ventricle. From there the blood is pumped out into the pulmonary artery and then to the lungs, where it picks up oxygen and is cleansed of carbon dioxide.

A series of one-way *valves* (mitral, pulmonary, tricuspid, aortic) controls the blood flow through the heart and prevents blood from seeping back into the heart after it contracts. When the heart is empty and in its resting phase (*diastole*), it fills up again with oxygenated blood from the lungs and deoxygenated blood from the body.

The Heart.

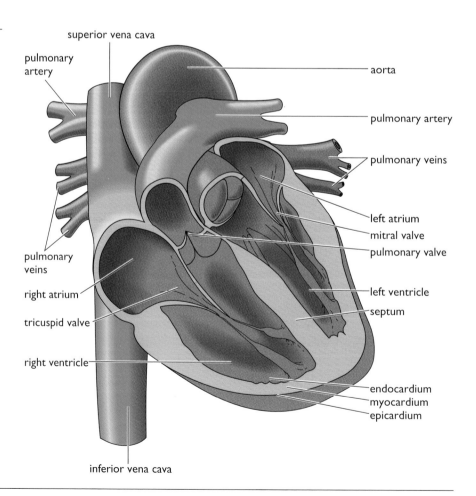

superior vena cava
pulmonary artery
aorta
pulmonary artery
pulmonary veins
left atrium
mitral valve
pulmonary valve
left ventricle
septum
endocardium
myocardium
epicardium
pulmonary veins
right atrium
tricuspid valve
right ventricle
inferior vena cava

The Heart Cycle. *In the systolic phase, the heart is active. The left ventricle pumps oxygenated blood through the aorta to the tissues and organs of the body. At the same time, the right ventricle sends deoxygenated blood through the pulmonary artery to the lungs. In the diastolic phase, the heart is at rest. The left side of the heart fills with oxygenated blood from the lungs, and the right side fills with deoxygenated blood from the body.*

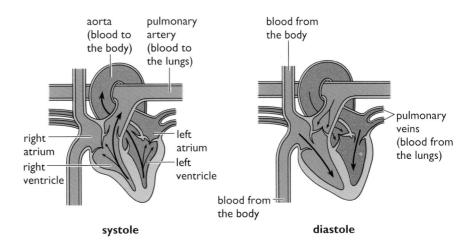

aorta (blood to the body)

pulmonary artery (blood to the lungs)

blood from the body

right atrium

right ventricle

left atrium

left ventricle

pulmonary veins (blood from the lungs)

blood from the body

systole

diastole

Your *heart rate*, the rate at which your heart beats and the amount of blood pumped with each contraction, increases at times of stress or during exercise to deliver more oxygen to the working muscles. A normal heart beats 60 to 80 times a minute while at rest. (Athletes' hearts may beat more slowly since athletes often develop larger hearts through training.) During exercise, when the muscles of the body demand more oxygen to perform, the heart rate may increase to 200 beats per minute. At rest, the heart pumps about 12 pints (about 6 L) of blood per minute, but during exercise it may increase its output to 100 pints (about 47 L) per minute. The heartbeat is regulated by natural electrical impulses that originate in a group of cells (known as the pacemaker) located in the wall of the right atrium. Sometimes this natural pacemaker fails to work properly and an artificial pacemaker must be surgically implanted to regulate the patient's heartbeat.

Common Heart Problems   During a routine physical examination, the physician may listen to your heart with a stethoscope. The normal, rhythmic "lubb" and "dubb" sounds are made by the closing of the heart's valves. Changes in the strength or clarity of these sounds may signal various diseases of the heart, lungs, or blood vessels. Myocardial infarction, commonly known as a *heart attack,* usually occurs when there has been a partial or complete blockage in one or more of the arteries that supply blood to the heart muscle. A *stroke* occurs when the flow of blood from the heart to the brain is cut off, depriving a section of the brain of oxygen. If your physician suspects that there is a problem with your heart, further tests will be conducted. (See also HEART ATTACK, **3**; HEART DISEASE, **3**; STROKE, **3**.)

How to Reduce the Risk of Heart Disease   Certain risk factors have been linked to heart disease. Some factors, such as age, sex, and heredity, cannot be controlled. Other factors—cigarette smoking, high blood cholesterol, hypertension (high blood pressure), stress, obesity, and lack of exercise, for example—can be modified through changes in diet and lifestyle as well as by good health care. Although there is no guarantee that you will not be affected by heart disease, you can make important personal choices that will lower your risk. (See also ATHEROSCLEROSIS, **3**; HYPERTENSION, **3**; HEART RATE, **4**.)

RISK FACTORS
▶ ▶ ▶ ▶ ▶ ▶

HEALTHY CHOICES

▶ **HIP**

The hip is the JOINT that connects the *femur*, or thighbone, to the PELVIS. It is a large *ball-and-socket joint* that allows the leg to make a wide range of motions. The hip bears the body's weight and works together with the knee and ankle joints to enable you to walk and run. The hip joint also enables your body to bend so that you can sit.

The femur and the three bones of the pelvis come together at the hip joint (see illustration: The Hip Joint). The rounded top of the femur fits snugly into the socket part of this ball-and-socket joint. Strong *tendons* and *ligaments* surround the hip joint, holding its bones firmly in place. Additional bands of ligaments attach the pelvis to the femur to control the extent of the joint's movement. The interior of the socket and the top of the femur are covered by smooth *cartilage*, which enables the ball to slide around in the socket. The joint is surrounded by a tough, fibrous capsule that cushions and lubricates the joint.

The Hip Joint.

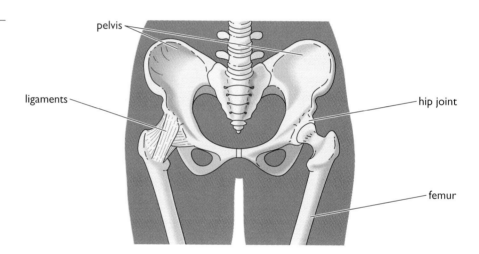

pelvis

ligaments

hip joint

femur

Common Hip Problems   Some infants are born with one or both hips dislocated—the rounded head of the femur does not fit into the socket and instead lies outside of it. This condition can be corrected by fitting the baby with splints for a few months, which will shift the femur into the socket. If the condition does not improve, surgery or traction—a system of weights and pulleys attached to the legs—may be advised.

The role of the hip joint in absorbing the strain of walking makes it especially susceptible to degenerative disorders, such as osteoarthritis and rheumatoid arthritis. Physicians may treat severe cases of arthritis by surgically replacing the entire hip joint with a metal or plastic prosthesis (see illustration: X ray of an Artificial Hip).

A fracture of the hip joint is rare. When people talk of a "broken hip," they are usually referring to a fracture of the top or neck of the femur. Some fractures of the femur may require the replacement of the head of the femur with an artificial ball that can be inserted into the socket of the joint. (See also CONNECTIVE TISSUE; MUSCULOSKELETAL SYSTEM; ARTHRITIS, **3**.)

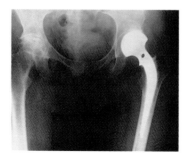

X ray of an Artificial Hip.   *This X ray shows an artificial hip joint in place after surgery.*

▶ HORMONE

A hormone is a chemical substance produced by a GLAND. Hormones regulate the growth, development, and metabolism of the body. They play an important role in digestion, in the reproductive system, and in the body's response to stress. Small amounts of hormones are constantly circulating in the bloodstream. They signal organs and tissues to perform chemical activities necessary to the normal functioning of the body.

Hormones are secreted by the glands that make up the ENDOCRINE SYSTEM (see chart: What Hormones Do). The function of hormones is to stimulate a reaction in specific parts of the body called *target tissues* or *target organs*. One hormone may stimulate liver activity, while another acts on certain cells in the bloodstream.

WHAT HORMONES DO		
Source	**Hormone**	**Function**
Pituitary	Human growth hormone	Stimulates growth; regulates metabolism
	Prolactin	Stimulates milk production
	Thyroid-stimulating hormone (TSH)	Stimulates hormone production in thyroid gland
	Follicle-stimulating hormone (FSH)	Stimulates function of ovaries and testes
Hypothalamus	Oxytocin	Stimulates contraction of uterus during childbirth
Thyroid	Thyroid hormone	Stimulates metabolic rate; regulates growth
	Calcitonin	Regulates level of calcium in the blood
Parathyroid	Parathyroid hormone	Increases level of calcium in the blood
Adrenal	Epinephrine	Fight-or-flight response
	Aldosterone	Regulates levels of sodium and phosphate
Pancreas	Insulin	Regulates level of blood sugar
Testes	Testosterone	Affects development of male sexual characteristics

Each hormone works to maintain a particular level of activity in its target tissue. The ADRENAL GLANDS, for instance, secrete the hormone *aldosterone*, which stimulates the kidneys to retain sodium (salt). When the body's sodium level falls too low, certain chemical messengers signal the adrenal glands to produce more aldosterone; when the sodium level rises too high, the adrenal glands are signaled to suppress the production of aldosterone.

Hormonal Disorders Most hormonal disorders, such as diabetes and Addison's disease, occur when a gland produces too much or too little of a particular hormone. Many hormones have been duplicated in the laboratory, however, enabling physicians to control certain hormonal disorders by supplying missing hormones or by counteracting excessive hormonal production. (See also EPINEPHRINE; METABOLISM; THYROID DISORDERS, 3.)

▶ HYPOTHALAMUS

The hypothalamus is a small but vital part of the BRAIN located at the top of the brain stem behind the eyes. It coordinates the functions of the NERVOUS SYSTEM and the ENDOCRINE SYSTEM. The hypothalamus also controls the nerves that regulate involuntary muscles and internal body organs.

The hypothalamus interprets signals from the nervous system and then activates the endocrine, or hormonal, system. For example, if special nerve cells called receptors send signals through the nervous system to the brain that certain HORMONES are needed by the body, the hypothalamus stimulates the body to produce those hormones. It does this by sending hormones called releasing factors to the PITUITARY GLAND, which is located directly below the hypothalamus. The pituitary gland then releases its hormones to the part of the body that needs them.

In some cases, the hypothalamus may direct the pituitary to activate other endocrine glands. For example, when the brain senses danger, the hypothalamus signals the pituitary to stimulate the adrenal glands to secrete, or release, the hormone epinephrine. EPINEPHRINE acts on the heart, lungs, and arteries to prepare the body to cope with the danger.

In addition to these functions, nerve cells in the hypothalamus receive information about body temperature, blood sugar, and other body conditions. The hypothalamus accordingly sends out instructions to regulate body temperature, hunger, thirst, sleep, emotions, and sexual urges.

The hypothalamus can be affected by emotional disorders, tumors, serious illnesses, and drug abuse. A malfunctioning hypothalamus can lead to extreme weight gain or loss, inability to control body temperature, disrupted menstrual cycles in women, and erratic sleep and sex patterns.

▶ IMMUNE SYSTEM

The immune system is a collection of specialized cells, structures, and substances that protect your body from disease and infection. It offers three levels of defense: the skin and mucous membranes, the inflammatory response, and immunity.

The Skin and Mucous Membranes The SKIN and MUCOUS MEMBRANES are the first line of defense. The skin forms a barrier against invading *pathogens*, which are disease-causing microorganisms. To enter the body, a pathogen must find a way through a cut in the skin or through one of the body's openings such as the mouth, eyes, nose, or vagina. The structures and substances in the mucous membranes that line the openings offer still further protection. A chemical in the sticky mucus can kill bacteria, and the tiny hairlike structures in the membranes of the nose and trachea (windpipe) can trap and filter out pathogens.

The Inflammatory Response.
A splinter can set the inflammatory response into action: The skin around the injured tissue becomes red and inflamed. Phagocytes rush to the area to engulf and destroy any bacteria or other pathogens that enter the wound.

The Inflammatory Response   If a foreign object—for example, a splinter, chemical substance, or infectious microorganism—gets past the first line of defense and enters the body, the second line of defense takes over. The inflammatory response is a general means of defense that occurs in the blood and tissues.

Once the foreign object has entered the body, the blood supply to the affected area increases, and the circulation in the area slows. This increases blood pressure in the area, causing fluid from the blood vessels to leak into the cell spaces near the object. Special proteins help defend against the invader. At the same time, phagocytes speed to the area to combat bacteria and other microorganisms. A *phagocyte* is a type of white blood cell that is central to the inflammatory response. The word *phagocyte* means "a cell that eats," and the phagocyte does just that. It encircles an invading microorganism, takes it apart, and "eats" it (see illustration: The Inflammatory Response).

If the infection or "invasion" is localized, that is, limited to one part of the body, you may be able to see the inflammatory response. For example, if you fall and scrape your knee or are stung by a bee, you will experience redness, swelling, and warmth at the site of the scrape or sting.

However, if the infection or invasion spreads throughout the body—as happens with certain bacteria and viruses—then the inflammatory response is more generalized and may result in a fever. A *fever,* marked by a higher-than-normal body temperature, aids the fight against disease. It signals the body to produce even more white blood cells and may even kill the invader, since many disease-causing organisms cannot survive in higher body temperatures.

Immunity   If the invader succeeds in overriding the second line of defense, the body's third line of defense, immunity, is put into action. It is effective against pathogens, such as bacteria and viruses. Again, white blood cells are used. One type of white blood cell that plays a major role in the body's immune system is the *lymphocyte,* which originates in the LYMPHATIC SYSTEM. There are two types of lymphocytes: B cells and T cells. The *B cells* are formed in bone marrow (thus the letter *B* is used). B cells produce *antibodies* that fight against and destroy invading pathogens. The production of antibodies is triggered by certain chemicals called *antigens* that are part of the pathogen. The B cells create specific antibodies to match the specific antigens. Once activated, the antibodies "hook up" to the antigens they were created for, helping to disable the invading pathogen.

If the invaders are viruses, the antibodies prevent them from entering healthy cells and causing damage. If the invaders are bacteria, the antibodies attach themselves to the bacteria and clump them together. This makes it easier for the phagocytes to surround and eat them. In addition, the antibody-bacteria clumps activate the production of bacteria-killing substances in the blood.

T cells start out in the thymus gland (thus the letter *T*). Some of them signal the phagocytes to eat faster. Others increase production of the antibodies produced by B cells. In addition, T cells attack foreign cells, such as those in a transplanted organ, and cells that have already been killed. It is believed that T cells may also attack cancer cells, but our understanding of this process is still not complete.

Types of Immunity   There are two types of immunity: natural (or innate) immunity and acquired immunity. Natural immunity is what you have during infancy: A newborn inherits some defenses against disease from the mother during pregnancy and gains other defenses through breast-feeding.

However, as children grow, they are exposed to pathogens that can get past the natural immunity and cause disease. If you develop measles, for example, your body will defend itself by producing measles-fighting antibodies. After the disease has passed, your body will have acquired an immunity to measles. If you are exposed to measles again your body will be able to fight it off immediately. Acquired immunity, then, develops as a result of exposure to various disease-causing organisms.

Immunity to specific diseases can also be acquired through *immunization*. Immunization involves the introduction of a small, harmless sample of disease-causing organisms into the body. The sample is too small to cause the disease to develop but large enough to cause the body to develop antibodies, and thus to acquire immunity, to the disease. For certain diseases, such as tetanus, booster shots are needed from time to time.

Immune System Disorders   When the immune system fails to respond or responds in an inappropriate way, people may experience allergic reactions to certain substances. More serious problems such as cancer or acquired immunodeficiency syndrome (AIDS) can also overwhelm the immune system.

Immunodeficiency diseases include a broad group of conditions that develop when the body cannot defend itself completely or in part from pathogens. People with immunodeficiency diseases have an immune system that either destroys white blood cells or decreases their production in the body. This leaves the body unprotected against bacteria and viruses and unable to fight them once they take hold. Some of these conditions are present at birth and may take years to show up. Others develop through exposure to various viruses. AIDS, for example, is caused by the human immunodeficiency virus (HIV).

Immunotherapy   Immunotherapy is used to modify the body's immune system. Often, people with allergies receive progressively stronger doses of a substance that enables them to build up tolerance for whatever triggers

Breast-feeding. *Breast milk provides the newborn baby with important antibodies to fight disease.*

the allergic response. Certain drugs called immunosuppressive drugs are used after organ or tissue transplant surgery to prevent the body from fighting the foreign cells of the transplant.

Ensuring Immunity   Regular immunizations for infants and children as well as scheduled boosters for adults can help ward off certain diseases. Good diet, exercise, limited stress, and enough sleep can help strengthen your body as well as your immune system. (See also AIDS, **2**; ANTIBODY, **2**; ANTIGEN, **2**; FEVER, **2**; IMMUNITY, **2**; IMMUNIZATION, **2**; AUTO-IMMUNE DISORDER, **3**; IMMUNOTHERAPY, **3**.)

HEALTHY CHOICES
▪ ● ● ● ● ● ● ● ● ● ● ● ▪

▶ INTESTINES   see DIGESTIVE SYSTEM

▶ JAW

The jaw is the portion of the SKULL that anchors the teeth and enables you to talk, bite, and chew. The upper jaw, the *maxilla*, is an immobile part of the skull. The lower jaw, the *mandible*, is the only movable bone of the skull; it is attached to the skull just below the ears at the temporomandibular joints. These *hinge joints* enable the jaw to open and close and make side-to-side movements (see illustration: The Jaw).

A sudden hard blow can cause the jaw to become dislocated or fractured. A dislocated jaw may need to be reset by a physician. Temporomandibular joint (TMJ) syndrome is a condition often caused by arthritis in which the joint is misaligned. Symptoms of TMJ syndrome include jaw pain and headaches. (See also MOUTH; TOOTH; TEMPOROMANDIBULAR JOINT SYNDROME, **3**.)

The Jaw.

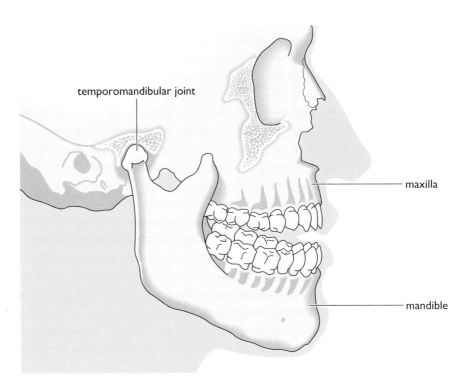

temporomandibular joint

maxilla

mandible

▷ **JOINT**

A joint is the site at which two bones meet. The primary function of joints is to enable movement. There are several types of joints allowing different ranges of motion. *Ball-and-socket joints* at the SHOULDERS and HIPS permit the arms and legs to make a wide range of movements (see illustration: Ball-and-Socket Joint). The *pivot joint* that links the SKULL to the spinal column enables the head to rotate from side to side. *Hinge joints* at the ELBOWS, KNEES, and fingers allow the bones on each side to bend and straighten.

Ball-and-Socket Joint. (a) *Ball-and-socket joints at the shoulders make it possible to move the arms in many directions.*

Structure of the Elbow. (b) *The elbow is a complex hinge joint. Like all hinge joints, it can bend and straighten, but the elbow joint can also rotate the arm from side to side.*

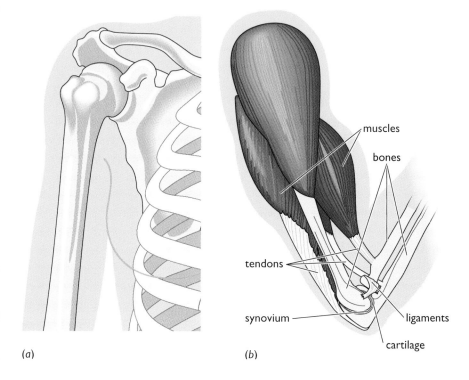

muscles

bones

tendons

synovium

ligaments

cartilage

(a)

(b)

A Typical Joint The ends of the bones that meet in a joint are covered with smooth *cartilage*. The space between the bones is lined with a membrane called a *synovium* that secretes a thick, slippery fluid. This fluid lubricates the joints and reduces friction between the bones. When you contract the MUSCLES and *tendons* on each side of a joint, you cause the bones in the joint socket to move. At the same time, the ligaments stretching across the joint prevent too much movement (see illustration: Structure of the Elbow).

Joint Injuries Joints are especially prone to injuries because they can be moved only in certain directions. Damage to joints, such as torn ligaments or sprained tendons, is particularly common among athletes. Many sports-related injuries can be avoided, however, by stretching and warming up the muscles and joints before starting to exercise. The usual remedy for minor injuries is RICE (rest, ice, compression, and elevation), but severe injuries may require surgery. Diseases such as osteoarthritis and rheumatoid arthritis can damage bones and deform joints. (See also CONNECTIVE TISSUE; MUSCULOSKELETAL SYSTEM; ARTHRITIS, 3; SPORTS INJURIES, 4.)

▶ KIDNEY

Located in the back of the abdominal cavity, the kidneys play a key role in the body's EXCRETORY SYSTEM. You have two of these bean-shaped organs (see illustration: The Kidneys). Their main function is to filter out extra water and waste substances from the blood. Even though this waste is produced by the normal functioning of the body, the body must dispose of it to remain healthy. The kidneys also regulate the level of sodium and water in the blood.

The Kidneys. (a) *Location of the kidneys.* (b) *Each of the hundreds of thousands of nephrons in a kidney is made up of a glomerulus (pl. glomeruli) containing a cluster of capillaries and a tubule. In the nephron, blood is filtered and substances that the body needs are reabsorbed into the blood. Excess water and the substances that remain are urine.*

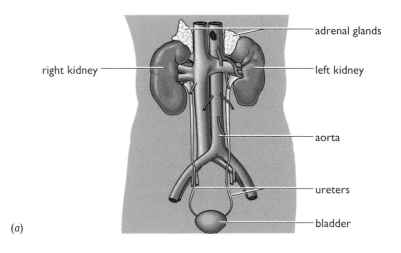

(a)

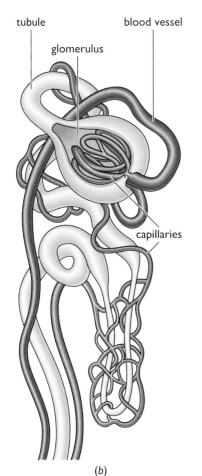

(b)

Structure of the Kidneys   Each kidney contains a vast network of blood vessels, a collecting area for urine, and about a million nephrons. A *nephron* is a microscopic filtering system made up of a *glomerulus* (a cluster of tiny capillaries), enclosed in a capsule of membrane, and a tubule (a long, narrow tube). Arteries and veins in the kidney branch into smaller and smaller blood vessels leading to the capillaries in the glomerulus. It is in these capillary clusters that waste substances are filtered out of the blood. Extending from the glomeruli are tubules that lead to the area of the kidney where urine is collected. *Urine* consists of excess water and dissolved matter.

How the Kidneys Work   Blood flows under pressure into the minuscule capillary clusters in the nephrons, forcing small-molecule wastes through their thin walls. Because blood cells and most nutrients are too large to move through the capillary walls, they remain in the blood. The waste fluid flows into the tubules, but capillaries around each tubule reabsorb the water, calcium, sodium, and other minerals the body needs. What remains is *urine*, which then flows to the collecting area of the kidney. Finally, the urine passes from the kidney to the bladder through a tube called the *ureter.*

When you drink large quantities of liquid, your kidneys will produce more urine; if you lose water through perspiration, your kidneys will produce less urine. The kidneys also adjust the acidity and amount of sodium of the urine to keep your body's chemistry in balance. The ADRENAL GLANDS, which sit above the kidneys, aid in this process by producing a hormone that controls the sodium in the urine. The kidneys also produce their own hormones as well as some ENZYMES, substances that trigger chemical reactions. These chemical reactions help the body make and distribute red blood cells and regulate blood pressure.

Common Kidney Problems   If calcium or certain other substances build up in the kidneys, *kidney stones* may form. Kidney stones can often be controlled by drinking plenty of fluids and limiting calcium in the diet. *Hypertension,* or high blood pressure, can damage the tiny blood vessels within the kidneys. A low-salt (low-sodium) diet is generally advised for people who are likely to develop hypertension. If lifestyle changes and medication do not successfully resolve these or other kidney problems, eventually the kidney will fail. Fortunately, a person can live a healthy life with one functioning kidney. (See also URINARY TRACT; HYPERTENSION, **3**; KIDNEY DISORDERS, **3**.)

▶ KNEE

The knee is the large JOINT that connects the long bones of the leg: the *femur* (thighbone) and the *tibia* (shinbone). Along with the hip and ankle joints, the knees enable the legs to bend so you can walk and run. The knee is a *hinge joint,* a type of joint that bends and straightens. When the *hamstring muscles* in the back of your thigh contract, the knee bends; when the *quadriceps muscles* in the front of your thigh contract, the knee straightens.

The front of the knee is covered by strong tendons extending from the thigh muscles to the top of the tibia. Tendons also hold the patella (kneecap) in place. The *patella* is a flat bone at the front of the knee that protects the knee joint. Cartilage covers and pads the ends of the tibia and femur, making it easier for the bones to slide over one another. The synovial membrane encloses the joint in a fluid-filled capsule that lubricates the joint, reducing friction between the two bones. Additional fluid-filled sacs called *bursas* cushion the patella. Several strong ligaments run along the sides of the joint from the femur to the tibia. These ligaments prevent the leg bones from sliding sideways. Other ligaments inside the joint prevent the knee from bending and straightening too far (see illustration: Structure of the Knee).

Common Knee Problems   The knee is susceptible to injuries. Most injuries occur when the knee is twisted too far in any direction or when

Structure of the Knee.   *The structure of the knee helps protect it from injury. The tendons and ligaments strap the bones in place, and the bursas cushion and protect the joint from jarring injury.*

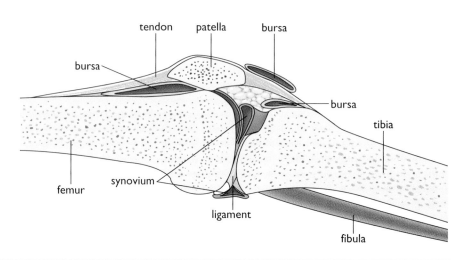

it is subjected to excessive pounding or overuse. Both are common in active sports such as football, basketball, and tennis. Common knee problems include *tendinitis* (inflammation of the tendons), *bursitis* (inflammation of the bursas), *runner's knee* (sprained ligaments), and torn cartilage. The knees are also vulnerable to joint disorders such as osteoarthritis and rheumatoid arthritis—painful degenerative diseases in which the bones and cartilage of the knee wear away.

HEALTHY CHOICES
● ● ● ● ● ● ● ● ● ● ● ●

How to Prevent Problems   Wearing kneepads during sports activities can help prevent knee injuries. Most knee injuries will heal well if the knee is rested, but serious injuries may require surgery. (See also CONNECTIVE TISSUE; MUSCULOSKELETAL SYSTEM; SPORTS INJURIES, **4.**)

▷ **LARYNX**   **see** THROAT

▷ **LIFE EXPECTANCY**   Life expectancy is a mathematical average of the number of years a group of people who are the same age will probably live. Life expectancy has been steadily increasing in the United States (see graph: Life Expectancy in the United States, 1920–1990). For example, a person who is about 50 years old today has a life expectancy of about 63 years. The life expectancy of a person born today is about 75 years. There are also differences in life expectancy between men and women as well as blacks and whites in the United States. Presently, white women have the highest life expectancy, 79.3 years. For black women, the figure is 76.3 years; for white men, 72.6 years; and for black men, 68.4 years.

Life Expectancy in the United States, 1920–1990.   *The graph shows how life expectancy at birth has changed since 1920.*

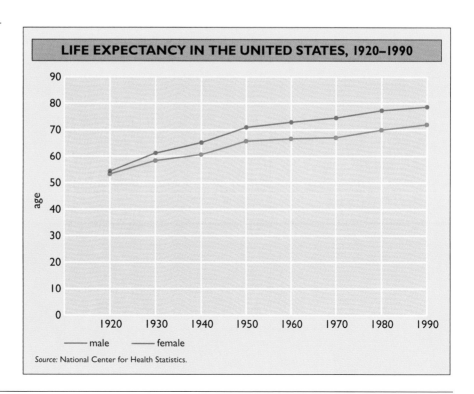

LIFE EXPECTANCY IN THE UNITED STATES, 1920–1990

— male   — female

Source: National Center for Health Statistics.

Life span, on the other hand, can have either of two meanings. *Maximum life span* is the number of years humans as a species are able to live. Many scientists think that few, if any, humans can live to be more than 120 years old. A person's *actual life span* is the number of years that person does, in fact, live. Although actual life spans vary greatly, an increasing number of Americans are living into their eighties and beyond. People age 85 and older make up the fastest-growing segment of society today.

There appear to be many reasons for these increases in actual life span and subsequent increases in life expectancy. Chief among them are medical advances, the control or elimination of some diseases, reduced infant mortality, and lifestyle changes.

Increasing Your Actual Life Span   Although life expectancy is a statistical figure that you cannot change, you do have considerable control over increasing your actual life span. Chances are good that if your relatives lived long lives, you will, too. Even if some of them did not, however, research is showing that good nutrition, exercise, preventive medical care, and an overall healthy lifestyle may not only lengthen your life but also improve the quality of your life. (See also LIFESTYLE, **4.**)

HEALTHY CHOICES

▶ **LIGAMENT**   **see CONNECTIVE TISSUE**

▶ **LIVER**

The liver is a large, complex organ that plays a key role in the DIGESTIVE SYSTEM. It has two principal functions: to digest and store nutrients from the food you eat and to remove or break down waste products or harmful

Location of the Liver.

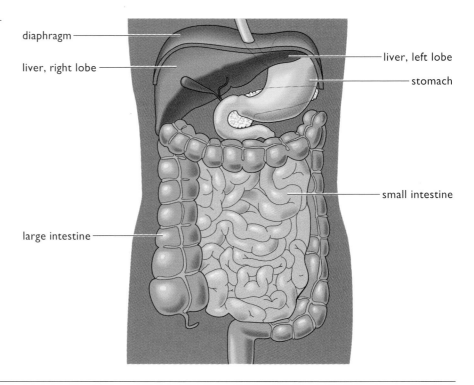

diaphragm

liver, left lobe

liver, right lobe

stomach

small intestine

large intestine

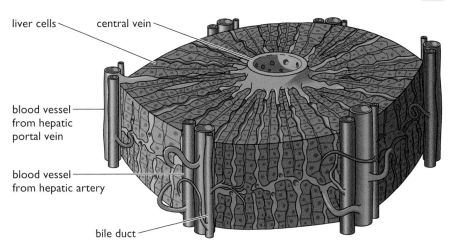

liver cells   central vein
blood vessel from hepatic portal vein
blood vessel from hepatic artery
bile duct

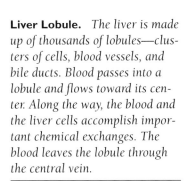

Liver Lobule. *The liver is made up of thousands of lobules—clusters of cells, blood vessels, and bile ducts. Blood passes into a lobule and flows toward its center. Along the way, the blood and the liver cells accomplish important chemical exchanges. The blood leaves the lobule through the central vein.*

substances in the blood. In addition, the liver stores energy, breaks down old blood cells, regulates body hormones, and produces proteins and chemicals that cause the blood to clot. The liver is located in the upper right part of the abdominal cavity (see illustration: Location of the Liver).

Structure of the Liver   The liver has two main sections, or lobes. Each lobe consists of thousands of *lobules*, which are clusters of liver cells, blood vessels, and bile ducts (see illustration: Liver Lobule). Two main blood vessels enter the liver. One, the hepatic artery, carries oxygenated blood from the heart to the liver cells; the other, the hepatic portal vein, brings nutrient-rich blood from the small intestine. Each branches into smaller and smaller blood vessels leading to the outside of the lobules. Inside the lobules, the cells are arranged in channels much like the spokes of a wheel, with space between the spokes for blood to flow.

How the Liver Works   Nutrient-rich blood flows from the outer edge of the cell clusters through the channels toward the center of the lobules. Various substances move into and out of the blood as it flows past the liver cells. The cells absorb and store some of these substances, such as glucose, iron, and vitamins, until the body needs them. Other substances, such as drugs and poisons, are broken down into waste products that become part of the bile secreted in the liver lobules. *Bile*, a greenish-yellow liquid, also contains salts that help the body digest fats. Bile is carried out of the liver through bile ducts and into the GALLBLADDER.

The liver cells produce other substances, such as cholesterol and blood proteins. These are secreted directly into the blood as it flows through the channels of the lobules. By the time the blood reaches the center of the lobule, numerous chemical exchanges have been completed and the blood leaves the lobules through the central vein.

Common Liver Problems   *Jaundice,* marked by a yellowness of the skin and eyes, results when bile pigments accumulate in the blood. This can be caused by a blocked bile duct or by liver diseases such as hepatitis that prevent the liver cells from processing bile correctly. *Hepatitis* is an inflammatory disease that is usually caused by a virus or alcohol or drug use. In alcoholism, the liver cells are so busy breaking down the alcohol that they can do little else. Eventually, this situation can lead to *cirrhosis,* a condition in which the cells are destroyed. Cirrhosis may also cause a buildup of excess fluid in the liver.

How to Prevent Liver Problems   The most important ways you can keep your liver healthy are to avoid alcohol and to use drugs only when medically necessary. A diet high in vitamins and minerals can also be extremely helpful. Limiting the amount of salt in your diet can minimize the chances of a buildup of fluid in your liver.

Unlike many other organs, the liver has the ability to regenerate lost tissue. Even if you lose as much as three-quarters of the liver to disease or surgery, the remaining cells can still carry out all the important functions of the liver. (See also HEPATITIS, **2**; CIRRHOSIS, **3**; JAUNDICE, **3**.)

▶ LUNG

The lungs are the main organs of the RESPIRATORY SYSTEM. Their principal function is to provide oxygen to the blood and to remove carbon dioxide from it. You have two lungs. They are suspended in the chest cavity where they are protected by the rib cage.

Structure of the Lungs   The lungs are soft, spongy organs containing millions of tiny air sacs. Layers of membrane called the *pleura* cover the lungs and the walls of the chest cavity. Lubricating fluid between these two layers enables the lungs to expand and contract easily as you breathe.

The air you inhale reaches your lungs by way of the *trachea* (windpipe). At the point where the trachea meets the lungs, it divides into two bronchial tubes (air passageways). Within the lungs, the bronchial tubes

Parts of a Lung.

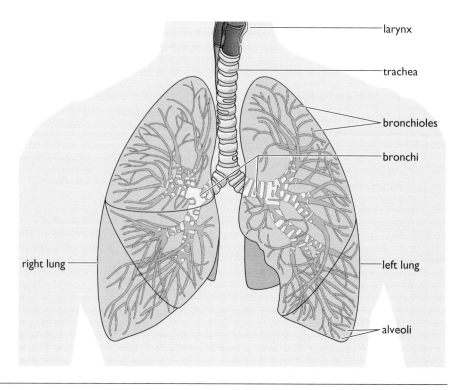

larynx

trachea

bronchioles

bronchi

right lung

left lung

alveoli

branch into smaller passageways called *bronchi,* which in turn narrow into still smaller tubes called *bronchioles.* Tiny hairlike structures called *cilia* line the airways and help trap disease-causing organisms. Finally, the bronchioles end in tiny air sacs called *alveoli* (see illustration: Parts of a Lung).

How the Lungs Work   The functioning of the lungs is closely linked with that of the CIRCULATORY SYSTEM. After your blood has traveled through your body, it returns to the heart and then by way of the pulmonary artery flows to the lungs. There the blood moves through smaller and smaller blood vessels until it reaches the tiny CAPILLARIES that line the alveoli. It is in the alveoli that carbon dioxide and oxygen are exchanged. Carbon dioxide is filtered out of the blood and replaced with oxygen. The blood then flows into progressively larger vessels until it reaches the heart. From there it is again pumped through the body, distributing oxygen to the cells. Meanwhile the carbon dioxide leaves your body when you exhale.

Common Lung Disorders   Several serious lung disorders—including chronic bronchitis, emphysema, and lung cancer—have been linked to cigarette smoking. Studies also show a connection between prolonged exposure to polluted air and lung disorders. *Chronic bronchitis,* an inflammation of the bronchial passages, develops when the airways in the lungs become narrowed and clogged with mucus. Usually this occurs because the cilia have been damaged and can no longer do their job. *Asthma* is a lung disorder characterized by narrowing of the airways, difficulty in breathing, and coughing. *Emphysema* develops when the lungs lose their ability to expand and contract properly. *Pleurisy* is an inflammation of the pleura.

Preventing Problems   You can keep your lungs healthy by avoiding cigarette smoke and pollutants and by getting plenty of exercise. (See also BRONCHITIS, **2**; ASTHMA, **3**; EMPHYSEMA, **3**; LUNG CANCER, **3**; LUNG DISEASE, **3**; PLEURISY, **3**.)

▶ **LYMPHATIC SYSTEM**   The lymphatic system collects fluid from tissues throughout the body and returns the fluid to the bloodstream. In this way the lymphatic system helps maintain a balance of fluids in the body. The lymphatic system also carries lipids, or fats, away from the digestive organs. In addition, the lymphatic system works with the IMMUNE SYSTEM by producing, storing, and circulating white blood cells to help the body fight disease and infection.

How the System Works   Fluid made up of water and other substances seeps through capillary walls into body tissue. This fluid, called *lymph,* nourishes the tissues and then is carried off by a network of lymphatic vessels. The vessels have a series of valves that prevent the lymph from flowing backward. The lymph vessels are connected to *lymph nodes,* bean-shaped organs of varying size. The main job of the lymph nodes is

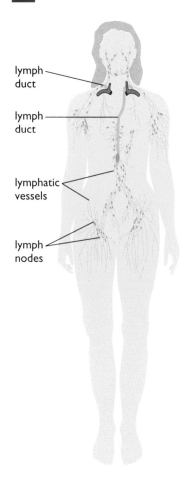

Parts of the Lymphatic System.

lymph duct

lymph duct

lymphatic vessels

lymph nodes

to collect and destroy microorganisms and foreign bodies such as dust traveling through the system.

After passing through lymph nodes located around the body, the lymph drains into the body's two lymph ducts (see illustration: Parts of the Lymphatic System). The lymph moves from the ducts into the bloodstream, becoming part of the blood plasma. It eventually reaches the heart and is recirculated throughout the body.

The lymph nodes help the body fight off infection and disease by filtering out bacteria and viruses before they can return to the bloodstream. While performing this function, they may become enlarged, which is why swollen lymph nodes, sometimes called swollen glands, are an indicator of infection. These nodes also produce and store white blood cells called *lymphocytes,* which play an important role in the body's immune system. Major lymph nodes can be found in the groin, armpits, neck, and chest. Masses of lymphoid tissue that have special disease-fighting functions include the TONSILS, ADENOIDS, and spleen.

Common Problems *Edema,* or swelling, may develop if the lymphatic system is blocked or not functioning well enough to carry fluid away from tissues. This sometimes happens in hot weather when, for example, the legs are not moved for a while and the lymph cannot drain from the tissues. In some women, swelling of the limbs also occurs in the days before menstruation.

The lymphatic system is sometimes responsible for the spread of cancer throughout the body. When a tumor grows to the point of invading the vessels carrying lymph, cancerous cells break off and are transported through the system. These cells then multiply to form a second tumor elsewhere and the process continues. (See also HODGKIN'S DISEASE, 3; LYMPHOMA, 3.)

▶ METABOLISM

Metabolism is the term used to refer to all the chemical processes that occur in your body. These processes are responsible for the repair and replacement of damaged or dead tissue, and they provide the body's energy.

How Metabolism Works Two basic types of metabolism are constantly taking place within your body. The first type is a process called *anabolism,* or constructive metabolism. Simple substances combine to form more complex ones, using up energy in the process. For example, simple amino acids combine to form a complex protein needed to help repair damaged tissues.

The second type of metabolism is a process called *catabolism,* or destructive metabolism. Complex substances are broken down into simpler ones, releasing both energy and heat. An example of this type of metabolism is the breaking down and eventual burning of glucose (sugar) in the body's cells to produce energy.

Control of Metabolism Both the rate and the type of metabolism going on in your body are controlled by HORMONES produced by your THYROID GLAND and your PANCREAS. Metabolism is measured in terms of *basal metabolic rate* (BMR). Your BMR is the amount of energy, measured in calories, needed to keep your body operating when you are at rest. Your BMR increases with activity and stress. Hundreds of metabolic disorders can result from too little or too much hormone production. These include diabetes and hypothyroidism (too little) and hyperthyroidism (too much). (See also BODY METABOLISM, **4.**)

▶ MOUTH

The mouth is the cavity formed by the upper and lower jaws. The mouth plays an important role in the digestive process. It also takes in air for the respiratory system and helps humans form the sounds necessary for speaking.

Structure of the Mouth   The *lips* are folds of flesh and muscle that ring the opening of the mouth. The movement of the lips facilitates speech. Lips also keep food and liquids in your mouth. The interior of the mouth and lips is lined with MUCOUS MEMBRANE, which lubricates and protects the surface of the mouth. Three sets of SALIVARY GLANDS in the floor and walls of the mouth produce *saliva*, which keeps the mouth moist and helps to break down food.

The roof of the mouth (the hard palate) and the lower jaw are lined with *teeth*, the hard, bonelike structures that enable you to chew and grind food. The teeth are embedded in the *gums* (gingivae), soft tissue that covers and protects the jawbones and nerves in the roots of the teeth. The *tongue* is a muscular, fleshy organ attached to the floor of the mouth. You use your tongue for speaking and also for tasting and mixing food so that it can be chewed, swallowed, and digested. The surface of the tongue is covered with tiny projections called taste buds that enable you to distinguish sweet, sour, bitter, and salty tastes in food. The tongue is rooted to the floor of the mouth by the lingual frenulum, a strong ligament running down the center of the underside of the tongue (see illustration: Parts of the Mouth).

Disorders of the Mouth   One of the most common disorders of the mouth is *gingivitis*, or inflammation of the gums. Gingivitis may occur if *plaque* builds up at the base of the teeth. Regular brushing and flossing prevents such a buildup. A sign of gingivitis is bleeding gums. If left untreated, gingivitis can lead to *periodontitis*, a serious gum disease. Another disorder of the mouth is *halitosis*, or bad breath. Like gingivitis, this is often caused by poor oral hygiene. Decaying teeth can also cause bad breath. In addition, certain foods—most notably onions and garlic—have a temporary effect on the breath.

The mucous membranes of the mouth and the surface of the tongue sometimes develop *ulcers*. These painful but usually harmless open sores usually clear up after a few days. The cause of mouth ulcers is unknown, but vitamin deficiency and stress may increase susceptibility. *Herpes simplex* is a virus that causes *cold sores*, or blisters, to develop on the lips or inside of the mouth. Cold sores normally clear up on their own but can recur. In rare cases, sores in the mouth are symptoms of tongue or mouth cancer. Any mouth sore that does not heal after three or four weeks should be examined by a physician.

HEALTHY CHOICES
●●●●●●●●●●●●●

CONSULT A

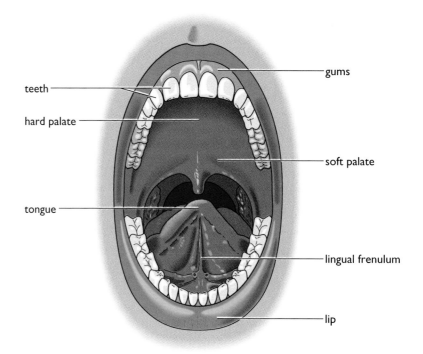

gums

teeth

hard palate

soft palate

tongue

lingual frenulum

lip

Parts of the Mouth.

HEALTHY CHOICES

Daily brushing and flossing are important oral hygiene practices to avoid tooth and gum diseases. You should also make a point of visiting your dentist regularly. (See also DENTAL EXAMINATION; TOOTH; COLD SORE, **2**; DENTAL PROBLEMS, **3**; GUM DISEASE, **3**.)

MUCOUS MEMBRANE

The mucous membrane is a thin sheet of protective cells that lines most of the cavities of the body. Mucous membranes contain millions of tiny glands that secrete *mucus,* a thick, slippery fluid. Mucus lubricates and protects the interior surfaces of the mouth, throat, eyelids, digestive tract, lungs, bladder, and vagina.

Mucous membranes in the nasal passages moisten incoming air. They also protect the body by trapping microorganisms and foreign particles and carrying them back to the throat, where they can be expelled by coughing or sneezing. In addition, mucus moistens and coats food so that we can taste, swallow, and digest it and protects the stomach wall from the corrosive effects of stomach acid.

MUSCLE

The human body has more than 600 muscles. These are the structures that enable the body to move and the internal organs to carry out their functions. Broad bands of muscles overlay and propel the skeleton. Other muscles form the walls of organs such as the heart, lungs, and stomach.

How Muscles Work Muscle is made up of a bundle of long, elastic fibers called myofibrils, and each bundle is surrounded by a strong sheath of CONNECTIVE TISSUE. Muscles are stimulated by nerves and by HORMONES that are secreted into the muscle cells.

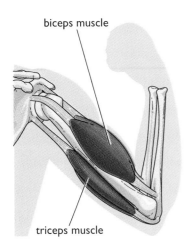

biceps muscle

triceps muscle

Using Muscles. *The biceps and triceps muscles form a pair. When you bend your arm, the biceps contracts and the triceps relaxes; when you straighten your arm, the triceps contracts and the biceps relaxes.*

A single muscle can only contract and relax. A pair of muscles, however, work together to provide movement. When one of the pair, the prime mover, contracts, the opposite muscle, the antagonist, relaxes. The *biceps* and *triceps* of the upper arm are a muscle pair. When the biceps contracts, the arm bends at the elbow. When the triceps contracts, the arm straightens (see illustration: Using Muscles). The contractions are controlled by nerves that carry messages from the brain to each bundle of muscle.

Kinds of Muscles   The human body has three kinds of muscles: voluntary muscles, involuntary muscles, and the cardiac muscle (see illustration: Kinds of Muscles). You use *voluntary muscles* to move parts of your body, such as legs or fingers. These muscles carry out orders from your brain, even though you may not always be aware of it. Voluntary muscles are called *striated* (striped) *muscles* because their muscle fibers are ringed by light and dark striped bands. The skeletal muscles are voluntary muscles that are attached to the bones by connective tissue called tendons.

Involuntary muscles are found in various organs, the skin, blood vessels, and glands. These muscles function automatically, without conscious control on your part. The fibers of the involuntary muscles are called *smooth muscles* because they have no striations, or stripes.

The major difference between the striated and smooth muscles is that the striated muscles can contract more quickly but the smooth muscles can remain contracted longer. The *cardiac* (or heart) *muscle* has characteristics of both kinds of muscles. It is an involuntary muscle, but its fibers do have striations. Your heart muscles contract about 100,000 times a day in order to send blood coursing through your circulatory system.

Muscle Disorders   *Muscular dystrophy* is a disease that causes the muscles to waste away. *Myasthenia gravis* weakens the muscles by interrupting the transmission of nerve impulses to the muscles. *Heart disease,* which attacks the cardiac muscle as well as the circulatory system, is a leading cause of death in the United States.

Overworked muscles may suffer such common injuries as strains, sprains, tears, and cramps. A *cramp* is a muscle spasm, a contraction that does not relax. Muscles become stronger and more flexible with regular use. Along with a proper diet, a program of moderate exercise several times a week builds strong muscles. Exercise also strengthens the heart. (See also MUSCULOSKELETAL SYSTEM; MUSCULAR DYSTROPHY, **3.**)

HEALTHY CHOICES
●●●●●●●●●●●●●

Kinds of Muscles. *The fibers of voluntary, or striated, muscles are ringed with light and dark bands. The fibers of most involuntary, or smooth, muscles have no such bands. The fibers of the cardiac muscle do have bands, but the heart is actually an involuntary muscle.*

voluntary muscle   involuntary muscle   cardiac muscle

▶ MUSCULOSKELETAL SYSTEM

The musculoskeletal system supports the body and enables it to move. It is made up of bones, joints, and muscles. BONES are a strong, hard material made of calcium, phosphorus, and other minerals. The bones connect with one another to form a framework, the *skeleton,* that surrounds the internal organs and gives the human body its basic shape. JOINTS are cushioned, flexible points at which the bones connect with one another. The joints act like hinges or pivots, allowing the bones on either side of them to move. The skeletal muscles are long, elastic fibers attached to the bones by *tendons.* In most cases, pairs of opposing muscles are attached to each bone. As the opposing

The Musculoskeletal System.
The adult human body contains approximately 206 bones and 650 muscles. Muscles and bones are connected by tendons.

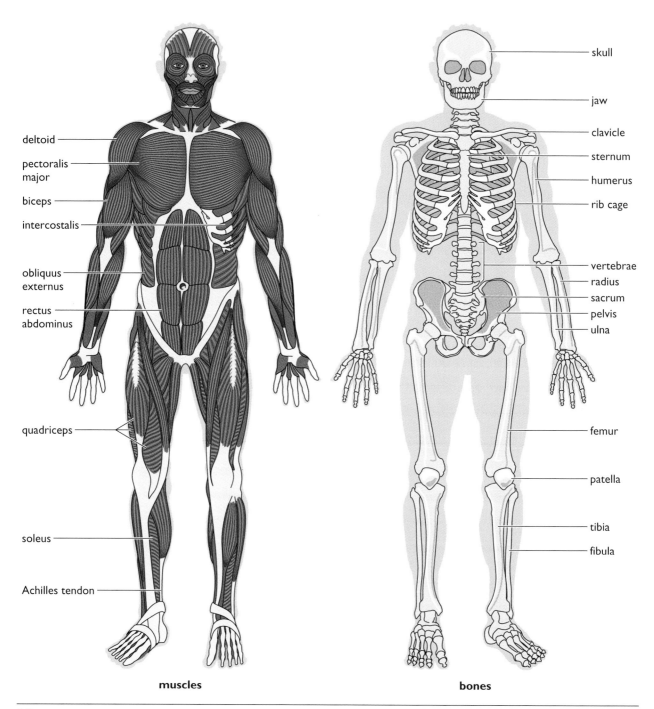

muscles   bones

muscles relax and contract, they cause the bones to move at the joints (see illustration: The Musculoskeletal System).

In addition to enabling the body to move, the musculoskeletal system protects the internal organs from injury. The SKULL encases the brain, the rib cage protects the heart and lungs, and the PELVIS supports the abdominal organs. The bone marrow in the cavities of bones produces many of the blood cells that are part of the circulatory system, which in turn provides nutrients to the muscles and bones.

Musculoskeletal Disorders Because of its role in protecting and animating the body, the musculoskeletal system is subject to many kinds of injuries. When bones are overstressed, they can fracture or break. Overtaxed muscles and tendons can suffer from tears, sprains, and strains. As people age, they may suffer from *arthritis*, the wearing away of bones or inflammation of joints, or from *osteoporosis*, the loss of calcium in the bones. Moderate, regular exercise can prevent or minimize many injuries to the musculoskeletal system. (See also CONNECTIVE TISSUE; EXERCISE, **4.**)

HEALTHY CHOICES
●●●●●●●●●●●●

▶ NAIL

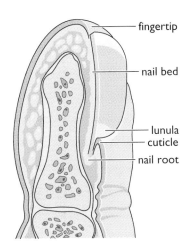

The Fingernail.

A nail is the hard, protective shell, or plate, at the tip of a finger or toe. The nails shield the soft tissue of the fingers and toes from injuries and help the fingers pick up very small objects. Nails are composed of *keratin*, the same protein that makes up the HAIR and SKIN.

A nail is dead tissue that contains no nerve cells or blood vessels. Nail tissue grows from a root located beneath a skin fold at the base of the nail (see illustration: The Fingernail). The *cuticle* is the top of the skin fold, and the *lunula* is the semicircular, whitish area at the base of the nail. It takes about six months for a fingernail and a year for a toenail to grow in completely from base to tip.

Nail Problems Hitting or crushing a nail can cause black spots of blood to form under the nail. Severe trauma to a nail may cause it to drop off eventually as a new one grows in. Small white patches are usually the result of minor injuries. Harsh chemicals may result in split or brittle nails. Fungal and bacterial infections can cause the nails to turn brown, yellow, green, black, or gray. These infections can be very difficult to treat.

The color and condition of the nails can also be a warning sign for some diseases. For example, anemia, psoriasis, or rheumatoid arthritis can make the nails pitted, ridged, or grooved. An *ingrown toenail* is a nail that curves under at the edge and grows into the flesh of the toe.

Nail Care Be sure to keep your nails clean and dry, and cut them every two or three weeks. File and shape any rough edges. Trim *hangnails*, pieces of cuticle that have become separated, with a nail clipper. Cut toenails straight across and wear properly fitting shoes to avoid ingrown toenails. When working in water or around chemicals, wear rubber gloves to protect the fingernails and skin. (See also FUNGAL INFECTIONS, **2**; FOOT PROBLEMS, **3.**)

HEALTHY CHOICES
●●●●●●●●●●●●

▶ NECK

The neck is the strong, slender structure that connects the skull and shoulders. It supports the head and enables it to move. Several important passageways connecting the head to the trunk pass through the neck. Food travels down the neck through the *esophagus,* and air reaches the lungs via the *trachea,* or windpipe. Seven *cervical vertebrae* of the spinal column are located in the neck. They surround and protect the SPINAL CORD, which passes through the neck. The head swivels on a *pivot joint* located between the first and second vertebrae.

Located in the neck are the *carotid arteries* and *jugular veins,* which carry blood to and from the head. The THYROID GLAND, located in the front of the neck, produces hormones that are essential for normal growth and development. The *larynx,* or voicebox, is also in the front of the neck. It enables you to speak. In addition, the neck contains a set of *lymph nodes* that trap infectious agents (see illustration: Parts of the Neck).

Parts of the Neck.

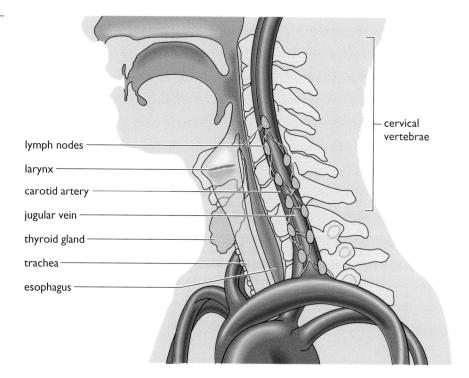

lymph nodes
larynx
carotid artery
jugular vein
thyroid gland
trachea
esophagus

cervical vertebrae

The structures of the neck are vulnerable to several common diseases such as colds, strep throat, and laryngitis. Another common problem is a stiff neck. A stiff neck can be caused by a sudden jerking of the head or by sleeping in an awkward position. Usually no treatment is needed. Sometimes, however, stiffness in the neck is a result of a degenerative disease, such as osteoarthritis. If a stiff neck persists, a physician should be consulted.

CONSULT A PHYSICIAN

A dislocation or fracture of any of the vertebrae in the neck is a serious injury. It can cause damage to the spinal cord, which can result in paralysis. The spinal cord can also be damaged by the whiplash injuries that sometimes result from automobile accidents. (See also RESPIRATORY SYSTEM; THROAT.)

> **NERVE**   see NERVOUS SYSTEM

> **NERVOUS SYSTEM**   The nervous system is the body's communication network. It gathers information from outside the body as well as from the various organs within the body. Then it processes that information and issues instructions to the muscles and glands. The nervous system enables humans to think, move, feel emotions, and interact with their environment. It coordinates the body's movements and functions so that various parts of the body can act in unison.

The nervous system is divided into two main parts (see chart: Parts of the Nervous System and illustration: Nervous System). The *central nervous system* consists of the BRAIN and SPINAL CORD. The *peripheral nervous system* is made up of 43 pairs of nerves that connect the brain and spinal cord to all other parts of the body.

How the Nervous System Works   The basic unit of the nervous system is the NEURON, or nerve cell. Neurons contain transmitting fibers, called axons, that send information from one neuron to the next throughout the central and peripheral nervous systems. The *nerves* that make up the peripheral nervous system are actually bundles of the axons of many neurons. Each nerve travels a certain path to or from a specific location in the body.

Some neurons, called *receptors*, are located in the sense organs (eyes, ears, skin, and so on). They receive information from the outside world. Receptor neurons in the skin, for example, receive information about pain, pressure, heat, cold, and touch. The information is transmitted, in the form of an electrical charge, along nerve pathways of sensory neuron fibers to the spinal cord and brain. These sensory neurons do not touch; each passes an electrical impulse to the next one along the

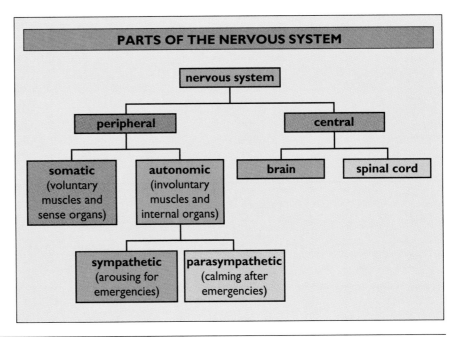

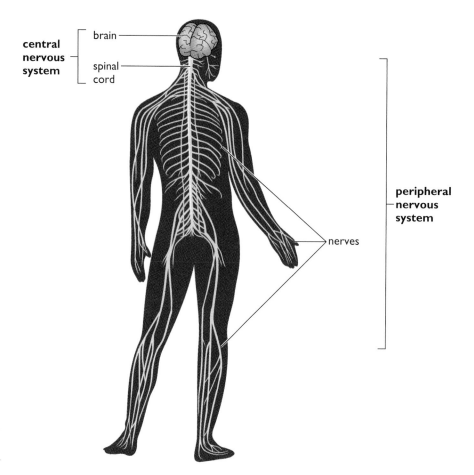

central
nervous
system

brain

spinal
cord

peripheral
nervous
system

nerves

Nervous System. *The human nervous system has two major parts: the central nervous system and the peripheral nervous system. The central nervous system consists of the brain and the spinal cord. The peripheral nervous system is composed of receptors in the sense organs, such as the ear, and nerves that connect the brain and spinal cord to all parts of the body. When the central nervous system receives information, in the form of electrical impulses, from the sense organs, it relays this information to the appropriate muscles and glands via the peripheral nervous system.*

pathway, across a *synapse*, or junction. (See also illustration: Neuron Structure and the Transmission of a Nerve Impulse in NEURON.)

When the impulse reaches the brain, the brain processes or interprets the information in much the same manner as a computer. Connecting neurons in the brain accept the sensory data and analyze it. Then they pass along instructions to motor neurons that carry the message back to the spinal cord and out along separate pathways of motor neuron fibers to the muscles. When a person feels cold, for example, the receptors send a message to the brain. The brain interprets the message as "cold" and sends out orders to the muscles to make the necessary moves for the person to put on a sweater. This process is known as *integration*.

The person in whom this process takes place is conscious of thinking, "I'm cold. I'll put on my sweater." That person is not necessarily aware of each and every message being sent to the muscles to carry out the act of putting on a sweater. Once a person learns a set of motions, such as standing, walking, and grasping, the circuits for those motions become so well developed that the motions can be performed with virtually no conscious control.

Not all messages go all the way to the brain. A *reflex arc* is a message that travels from the receptor to the spinal cord, which then sends its own instructions back to the muscles along the motor pathways in the same peripheral nerves. A "cold" message, for example, travels along its sensory pathway to the spinal cord, where it crosses over to connecting neurons that cause the spinal cord to send out orders to the muscles to shiver. Shivering is a REFLEX ACTION, an automatic muscular response to cold that generates body heat.

Autonomic and Somatic Nervous Systems The peripheral nervous system, which contains all the nerves of the body other than those of the brain and spinal cord, is divided into two main parts (see illustration: Peripheral Nervous System). The *somatic nervous system* contains all the nerves that serve the voluntary muscles and sense organs. The *autonomic nervous system* contains all the nerves that control involuntary muscles and internal organs such as the heart, glands, digestive tract, and arteries. The autonomic system is served by the *sympathetic nerves,* which prepare the body for emergencies, and by the *parasympathetic nerves,* which help the body relax after a crisis.

When a person is frightened or in danger, sympathetic nerves make the heart beat faster, constrict blood vessels to increase the blood supply to the muscles, and increase lung capacity. Then the body can respond efficiently to the threat it is facing. After the threat has passed, parasympathetic nerves cause the heart rate to slow, lower blood pressure, and open constricted blood vessels so that the body can return to its normal state.

The autonomic nervous system is also associated with emotional expression. When a person is nervous, for example, the autonomic nervous system stimulates the sweat glands, causing the person to perspire.

Disorders of the Nervous System The most common disorders of the nervous system are injuries such as a severed nerve or severed spinal

Peripheral Nervous System.
The peripheral nervous system has two main parts: the somatic nervous system and the autonomic nervous system. The autonomic system, in turn, is composed of sympathetic and parasympathetic nerves. Nerves of the somatic system serve the sense organs and voluntary muscles. Nerves of the autonomic system, which is directly involved in emotions, serve the involuntary muscles and internal organs, such as the heart and arteries.

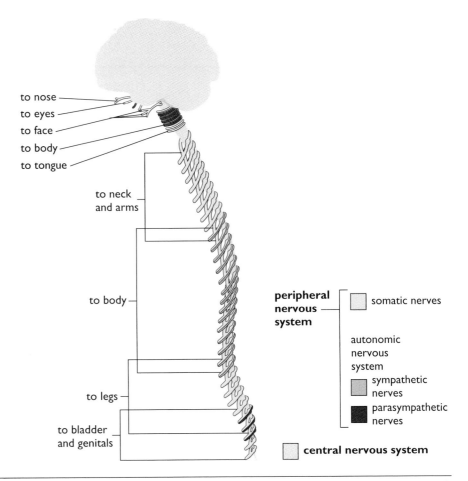

cord. These injuries can result in paralysis, loss of feeling, and loss of muscle control. Pinched nerves occur when something, such as cartilage or bone, presses on a nerve. A pinched nerve can be very painful, but the pain can be relieved through exercise, medication, or surgery.

Diseases, including multiple sclerosis and meningitis, can also damage the spinal cord and peripheral nerves. Damage to the sensory nerves can cause blindness, deafness, or a loss of sensation. Parkinson's disease, Alzheimer's disease, and brain tumors are disorders that destroy nerves in the brain and cause symptoms such as amnesia, tremors, and impairment of the thinking or memory functions. Medical specialists called *neurologists* treat nervous system disorders.

Preventing Nervous System Injuries   Avoid spinal cord injuries by always wearing a seat belt in an automobile and by never diving into shallow water. You can prevent brain injuries by wearing a helmet when riding a bicycle or motorcycle and when participating in certain sports, such as football. Excessive use of drugs and alcohol can damage brain cells. (See also AUTONOMIC NERVOUS SYSTEM, 5; CENTRAL NERVOUS SYSTEM, 5; PHYSICIANS (M.D.'s)—NEUROLOGIST, 9.)

HEALTHY CHOICES
●●●●●●●●●●●●

RISK FACTORS
▶ ▶ ▶ ▶ ▶ ▶

▶ NEURON

A neuron is a nerve cell, the basic unit of the nervous system. Within the NERVOUS SYSTEM, which is the communication center of the body, neurons are the "wires" that transmit information. Neurons carry the information in the form of electrical impulses to and from the brain and spinal cord through all parts of the body. These impulses enable the body to coordinate the functioning of organs and the movements of the body.

Main Types of Neurons   There are three main types of neurons. *Sensory neurons* carry impulses from the sensory organs, such as the eyes and ears, to the BRAIN and the SPINAL CORD. *Motor neurons* carry impulses from the brain and spinal cord to the muscles and glands. *Connecting neurons* are located within the brain and spinal cord. These neurons, the most plentiful type, connect with other neurons.

Neuron Structure   Each neuron is made up of three parts: a cell body, an axon, and dendrites (see illustration: Neuron Structure and the Transmission of a Nerve Impulse). The cell body receives and sends the electrical charges or impulses necessary for communication. It also maintains the cell's chemical processes and growth. An *axon* is a threadlike fiber that projects from the cell body. Its function is to send messages from the cell body to other neurons. Axons can range in length from a fraction of an inch to several feet, depending on their location in the body. Each axon can have several hundred smaller branches extending from it.

Dendrites are the neurons' message receivers. They, too, are threadlike and branched, but they are generally shorter than axons. Dendrites receive the electrical impulses and transmit them to the cell body. The point at which impulses travel from the axon of one neuron to the dendrite of another neuron is called a *synapse*. Axons have a round end called the synaptic knob. When an impulse reaches a synaptic knob, it releases *neurotransmitters*. These substances help the impulse travel from one neuron to another.

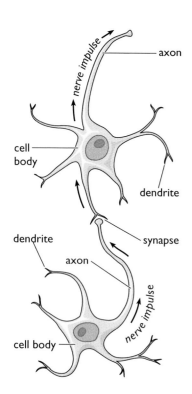

Neuron Structure and the Transmission of a Nerve Impulse.   *Arrows indicate the direction of the impulse from one neuron to another.*

Nerves are bundles of axons that travel to the same location. The sciatic nerve, for example, travels from the spinal cord all the way down the back of the leg.

Nerve Damage   Nerves may be cut completely or partially by an injury. Nerve fibers that are not completely severed may regenerate in some cases. In other instances, loss of muscle power or loss of sensation may occur. Surgery is the only treatment for nerves that are completely severed, and such surgery is not always successful. Pinched nerves occur when something, such as cartilage or bone, presses on a nerve. The pain from a pinched nerve may be relieved through exercise, medication, or surgery.

Nerves may also be damaged by disease, inflammation, vitamin deficiencies, drug side effects, and exposure to toxic substances such as mercury and lead.

▶ **NOSE**

The nose is the main gateway to the RESPIRATORY SYSTEM. When you breathe in, air enters through your nose and is filtered, warmed, and moistened before it continues on its route to the LUNGS. The nose is also the organ of smell. It helps you enjoy the taste of food because your sense of taste is largely dependent on your sense of smell.

Structure of the Nose   The bridge of the nose is formed by two small nasal bones. The rest of the external nose consists of flexible cartilage ending in the nostrils (see illustration: Structure of the Nose). Air entering the nostrils moves through the *nasal passage* (or cavity), located just above the roof of the mouth. This passage is divided into two identical passageways by a partition of bone and cartilage called the *septum*. The nasal passage also contains thin, curved pieces of bone that deflect and

Structure of the Nose.

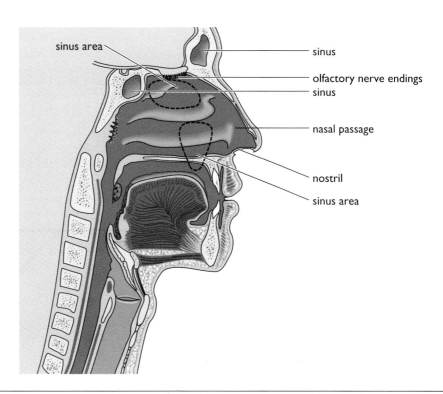

sinus area — sinus

olfactory nerve endings

sinus

nasal passage

nostril

sinus area

slow down the air. MUCOUS MEMBRANE and fine hairs line the surfaces of the nasal passage. The hairs filter out dust particles, and the mucous membrane warms and moistens the air and traps germs. The nasal passage leads to the upper throat. Mucus secreted by the mucous membrane carries germs and dust particles down to the throat, where they are swallowed or expelled by coughing. Also connected to the nasal passage are the SINUSES, eight air-filled cavities in the bones of the face.

The roof of the nasal passage contains *olfactory nerve* endings that sense odors and transmit information to the brain for processing.

Disorders of the Nose The nose's functions as a filter for germs make it vulnerable to several minor ailments. The most prevalent is the *common cold*, an infection of the respiratory tract caused by a virus. Bacteria and allergies can cause inflammations of the nose and sinuses.

CONSULT A
PHYSICIAN

A blow to the nose can break the nasal bones and damage the cartilage. Fractures that distort the alignment of the nose should be treated by a physician. A *deviated septum*, a misalignment of the partition that separates the nasal passages, can obstruct breathing and block openings to the sinuses. Many people occasionally have *nosebleeds*, a hemorrhage of a blood vessel in one of the nasal passages. To stop a nosebleed, pinch the bleeding nostril closed for 5 or 10 minutes. (See also ADENOIDS; COMMON COLD, **2**; NOSEBLEED, **3**.)

► PANCREAS

The pancreas, an eggplant-shaped organ in the back of the abdomen, is part of both the DIGESTIVE SYSTEM and the ENDOCRINE SYSTEM (see illustration: Location of the Pancreas). As a digestive organ, the pancreas helps the body break down foods. As an endocrine gland, it produces hormones that regulate glucose (sugar) levels in the blood.

How the Pancreas Works When food reaches your stomach, some of the cells of the pancreas begin producing juices. These juices flow into the main pancreatic duct and then into the small intestine. At this point, ENZYMES in the pancreatic juice are activated and start to break down proteins, carbohydrates, and fats in the small intestine. Pancreatic juice also contains bicarbonate, a substance that neutralizes the stomach acid it encounters in the small intestine.

Location of the Pancreas.
Located at the back of the stomach, the pancreas sits in the C-shaped curve of the upper portion of the small intestine. The pancreas is about 5 to 6 inches (about 13 to 15 cm) long.

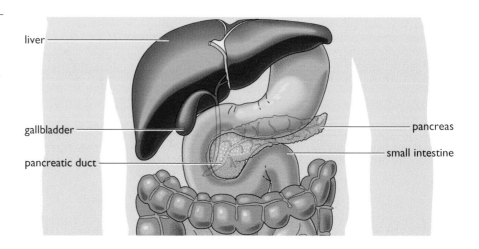

liver

gallbladder

pancreatic duct

pancreas

small intestine

The pancreas also contains tiny clusters of cells called the *islets of Langerhans*. These cells release two hormones, *insulin* and *glucagon,* which act as regulators of the level of glucose.

Disorders of the Pancreas   If the pancreas produces too little insulin or too much glucagon, *diabetes* can result. People who have *cystic fibrosis* do not produce a sufficient quantity of the pancreatic enzymes that break down foods. As a result, food passes through their system without giving up fats and other important nutrients. (See also CYSTIC FIBROSIS, **3**; DIABETES, **3**.)

▶ PELVIS

The pelvis is the skeletal structure that supports and protects the lower abdominal organs. These organs include the bladder, the large intestine, and the reproductive organs in women and the prostate gland in men. Several large muscles attach to the pelvis and, together with the pelvis, bear most of the body's weight. From the pelvis, the spinal column extends upward and the leg bones extend downward.

Each side of the pelvis is made up of three bones: the ilium, the ischium, and the pubis (see illustration: The Pelvic Bones). These bones are separate in childhood but fuse as the body matures. The ilium (hipbone) is the large, flat bone that protrudes slightly just below the waist at either side of the hip. It joins the *sacrum* at the *sacroiliac joints*. The ilium, the ischium, and the pubis come together on each side of the body at the hip joint. The *hip joint,* a large *ball-and-socket joint,* is the place where the thighbone is attached to the body.

The structure of the pelvis differs slightly in men and women. The female pelvis is broader, creating a large pelvic cavity through which an infant can pass during childbirth. The male pelvis is heavier and can support greater weight.

It takes great force to fracture the pelvis. Pelvic breaks usually heal well on their own, but surgery may be required to repair any damage to the internal organs. Repetitive actions, such as kicking a ball, sometimes cause inflammation of the joint at the front of the pelvis (pubic symphysis). This condition, which affects soccer players, usually disappears with rest. (See also HIP.)

The Pelvic Bones.   *The ilium (hipbone) meets the spinal column at the sacrum, a section of fused vertebrae in the lower back. The ischium curves around to form the bone structure of the buttocks. The two pubis bones join at the pubic symphysis.*

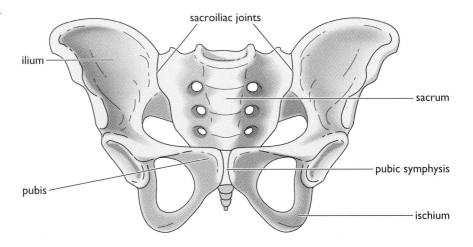

▶ PHYSICAL EXAMINATION

A physical examination usually consists of a three-part medical consultation that provides a physician with information about a person's health. The exam typically includes taking a medical history, examining organs and parts of the body, and ordering laboratory tests. The purpose of a physical exam is to check on a person's overall health or to diagnose and prescribe treatment for an illness or injury.

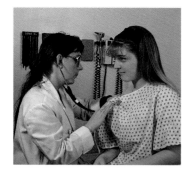

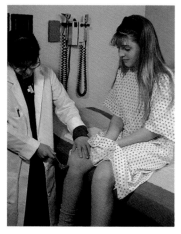

The Physical Examination.
Regular routine physical examinations help people maintain their health by detecting any medical problems early enough so that they can be treated promptly and successfully.

Medical History In taking a medical history, a physician or other health-care professional asks about past illnesses, serious injuries, operations, immunizations, allergies, and any medications currently being taken. The physician also wants to know about any diseases that occur in the patient's family. If a specific medical problem has caused a patient to come in, the physician will want to know how long he or she has had the complaint and will ask specific questions about symptoms and treatment to date.

Perhaps most important, the physician will ask questions about the patient's lifestyle (sleep patterns, diet, exercise, stress levels, smoking and drinking habits). You can contribute a great deal to a physical examination by being frank and honest about your health.

The Examination When the exam is a well-care checkup or if the patient complains of generalized symptoms, the physician examines the whole body thoroughly. This includes measuring height and weight, taking BLOOD PRESSURE, and examining the eyes, ears, nose, mouth, teeth, and gums. The physician uses a stethoscope to listen to the heart and to check for abnormal sounds in the lungs and abdomen. He or she feels the thyroid and neck area to check for enlarged lymph nodes and examines the abdomen to look for hernias and to check the liver and spleen. Reflexes are tested by tapping the knees or ankle with a small rubber hammer.

When examining teenagers, physicians may pay special attention to medical "trouble spots" for teens. This involves carefully checking the eyes for nearsightedness; the ears for hearing problems; the mouth for gum disease; the spine for curvature; and the skin, thyroid gland, and lymph nodes for signs of infection or cancer. Adolescent girls usually receive a complete pelvic exam and Pap test as well as instruction in conducting a monthly breast self-examination. Boys may be examined for genital abnormalities and learn about testicular self-examination.

Laboratory Tests Although recommended routine laboratory tests depend on a person's sex, age, and medical and personal history, a physical examination usually includes a URINALYSIS and BLOOD TESTS and may also include an X ray of the chest. For adolescents, these tests screen for iron-deficiency anemia, high cholesterol levels, diabetes, and kidney disease. Additional tests are recommended as people get older, including electrocardiograms, rectal exams, and, for women, Pap tests and mammograms.

Frequency of Physical Examinations The recommended frequency for routine physical examinations varies considerably. The generally recommended frequency for teenagers is every one to two years. People with long-term health problems may need to see their physicians more often. It is also a good idea to have a physical examination before starting to play a new sport to detect any bone or joint problem or medical condition that could affect participation. (See also ELECTROCARDIOGRAM, **3**; EYE TEST, **3**; X-RAY EXAMINATION, **3**; GYNECOLOGICAL EXAMINATION, **6**; MAMMOGRAM, **6**; PHYSICIANS (M.D.'s), **9**.)

▶ ## PINEAL GLAND

The pineal gland is a small structure near the center of the BRAIN. It secretes the hormone *melatonin* during the hours of darkness and suppresses melatonin production when it is light outside. No one knows exactly what melatonin does, but researchers believe that it may regulate a person's circadian rhythm (24-hour cycle) or "internal clock."

The pineal gland is also believed to affect the onset of puberty. When melatonin production is suppressed in early puberty, the body delays sexual maturation. A tumor on the pineal gland can affect melatonin production, but such tumors are rare. (See also CIRCADIAN RHYTHM, **5**.)

▶ ## PITUITARY GLAND

The pituitary gland is part of the ENDOCRINE SYSTEM, a group of glands that secrete HORMONES into the bloodstream. The pituitary is often called the *master gland* because its hormones regulate the function of other endocrine glands as well as many body processes. Located at the base of the brain, the pituitary gland is a pea-size structure protected by a circle of bone (see illustration: Location of the Pituitary Gland). A stalk connects the pituitary gland with a part of the brain called the HYPOTHALAMUS. The

Location of the Pituitary Gland.

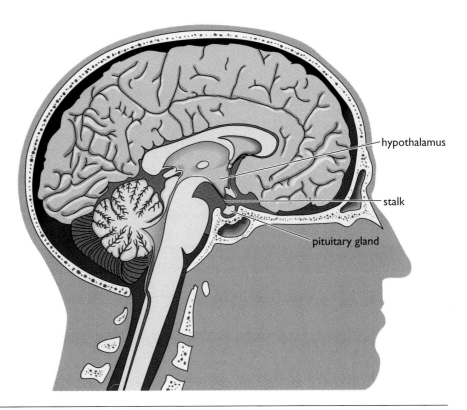

hypothalamus

stalk

pituitary gland

HORMONES OF THE PITUITARY GLAND

Hormone	Area(s) of action	Actions
Growth hormone	Skeleton, kidneys, liver, fat tissue	Stimulates growth, especially of bone and cartilage
TSH	Thyroid gland	Regulates the thyroid gland, which is involved in metabolism
ACTH	Adrenal glands	Stimulates glands to secrete hormones affecting metabolism
Prolactin	Female breasts	Stimulates breast development and, during breast-feeding, the production of milk
LH and FSH	Male and female sex organs	Controls the development and function of the sex organs
ADH	Kidneys	Regulates the amount of water in the body
Oxytocin	Female breasts, uterus	Stimulates contractions of the uterus during childbirth and the release of milk during breast-feeding
MSH	Skin and pigment cells	Determines the color of the skin

hypothalamus controls many activities of the pituitary gland and produces some of the hormones that the pituitary releases.

Hormones Produced by the Pituitary Gland The pituitary gland has three parts: the anterior, posterior, and intermediate lobes. Each lobe produces a range of hormones that stimulate other endocrine glands to manufacture their respective hormones (see chart: Hormones of the Pituitary Gland). The *anterior lobe* produces at least five important hormones. Growth hormone (GH) regulates size, primarily of the skeleton, and thyroid-stimulating hormone (TSH) controls the production of THYROID GLAND hormones, which are vital to body metabolism. Adrenocorticotropic hormone (ACTH) stimulates the adrenal glands to secrete hormones that also affect metabolism. Prolactin stimulates breast development in women, as well as milk production after childbirth. Finally, luteinizing and follicle-stimulating hormones (LH and FSH) help control the function of the reproductive organs in both men and women. The *posterior lobe* produces two hormones: antidiuretic hormone (ADH), which regulates the amount of water in the body; and oxytocin, which stimulates contractions of the uterus during childbirth and the release of milk from the breasts during breast-feeding. The *intermediate lobe* produces one hormone: melanocyte-stimulating hormone (MSH), which controls darkening of the skin.

Disorders of the Pituitary Gland Both congenital and genetic disorders may affect the pituitary gland, resulting in the release of too much or too little of one or more hormones. Insufficient growth hormone, for example, leads to short stature. Other problems may be caused by pituitary tumors, impaired blood supply, birth injury, or head injury. Enlargement of the pituitary gland may affect vision, because the gland is close to the optic nerves.

Recent studies have shown that secretion of growth hormone increases during exercise and periods of deep sleep. Therefore, good sleeping and exercise habits will help promote healthy pituitary gland function. (See also ENDORPHINS; GROWTH; GROWTH DISORDERS, 3.)

▶ RECTUM

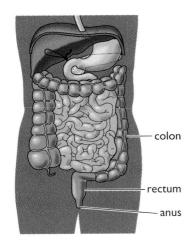

colon

rectum

anus

The Rectum.

The rectum is a short, muscular tube at the lower end of the colon (see illustration: The Rectum). Feces, undigested material and water, collect in this approximately 5-inch (about 13-cm) tube before passing through the ANUS during elimination from the body (defecation). The walls of the rectum have four layers. The three outer layers are composed of moist tissue cells, muscle, and supporting tissue, respectively. The innermost mucous layer lubricates the rectum.

When enough fecal matter has filled the rectum, it exerts pressure on the rectum's walls. This pressure causes impulses to be sent to the brain. The brain responds by signaling the anal muscles to relax, allowing the feces to leave the body.

Disorders of the Rectum   Because the rectum is basically an extension of the colon, similar problems affect both. Noncancerous growths known as polyps may form in the colon or the rectum. Familial polyposis involves the growth of polyps that may become cancerous. Cancer itself may also affect the rectum.

An infection or other problem may cause the rectum to narrow to the point where feces may not pass through. Rectal bleeding or discharge may occur because of injury of the rectal tissues during anal intercourse or insertion of foreign objects into the rectum.

During rectal examinations, physicians usually use either a proctoscope or a sigmoidoscope, two types of viewing tubes inserted into the rectum. These devices are used to detect and diagnose disorders of the rectum. (See also DIGESTIVE SYSTEM; COLORECTAL CANCER, **3**.)

▶ REFLEX ACTION

A reflex action is an automatic muscular response to a stimulus. If you shiver from the cold or drop a hot dish, you are experiencing a reflex action. Reflex actions occur instantaneously and without conscious thought. They are controlled by sensory and motor NEURONS, or nerve cells. The purposes of reflex actions are to protect the body from damage and to regulate certain essential physical activities such as breathing and temperature control. If you did not immediately drop a hot dish, your skin could be badly burned. When you shiver, the muscular action helps raise your body temperature to help protect it from the cold. Reflex actions are often followed by conscious thought. For example, after you unconsciously shiver, you may decide to put on a sweater to get warm.

How Reflex Actions Work   The simplest reflex action is the knee-jerk, or patellar, reflex. When the tendon of the muscle that straightens the knee joint is tapped, the tap stimulates a sensory neuron in the muscle. The neuron sends a message along the neuron pathway to the spinal cord. At the spinal cord, the message leaps across to a motor neuron that then sends the message along its neuron path back to the muscle. This signal causes the muscle to contract. When the muscle contracts, the lower leg jerks upward, and the knee straightens. This passage of the nerve signals is called a *reflex arc*. It takes place in a fraction of a second, without any conscious involvement of the brain.

More complicated reflex actions can involve more than one set of sensory and motor neurons and more than one muscle. If you reflexively avoid stepping on a piece of glass, for example, several sets of neurons and muscles are called into play to help your body change course and maintain its balance.

A *conditioned reflex* is one that has been learned. Hearing the word *dinnertime* may cause some people's salivary glands to increase the production of saliva. They have learned to associate the announcement of dinner with the pleasure of eating tasty food. People can also learn to hold off a reflex temporarily. For example, babies empty their bladder or bowels reflexively whenever either becomes full. After toilet training, however, children learn to prevent this reflex until they can get to a toilet. (See also HYPOTHALAMUS; NERVOUS SYSTEM.)

REPRODUCTIVE SYSTEMS

The reproductive systems are the male and female biological structures that enable humans to produce offspring. Males have the capacity to produce *sperm* (male cells) and place them inside women. Females have the capacity to become pregnant, give birth, and breast-feed their infants. Mature reproductive systems begin to develop at puberty. The age of onset of puberty varies but usually starts between 12 and 15 for boys and approximately 2 years earlier for girls.

Male Reproductive System.

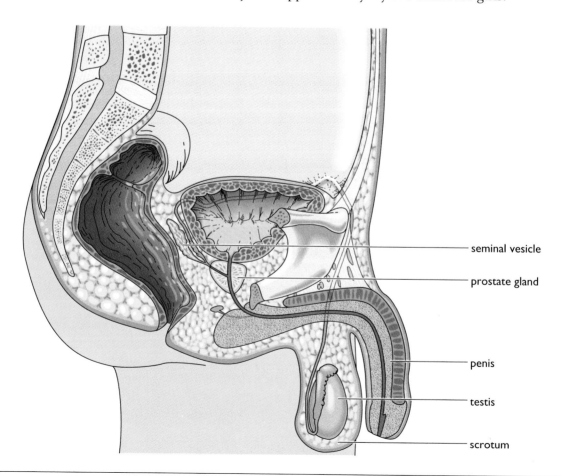

seminal vesicle

prostate gland

penis

testis

scrotum

The Male Reproductive System   The male reproductive system involves both external and internal structures (see illustration: Male Reproductive System). The *penis*, the organ sensitive to sexual arousal, and a sac called the *scrotum* are outside the body. The *testes* (sing. *testis*), or testicles, are two small glands that lie within the scrotum. Inside the pelvis are the seminal vesicles, various tubes, and the prostate gland.

Sperm are produced in the testes. A series of tubes store the sperm and connect the testes to the penis. The *seminal vesicles* and the *prostate gland* produce fluid that mixes with the sperm to provide *semen*. Semen can leave the body only when the penis is erect, which occurs when its spongy tissue fills with blood. *Ejaculation,* caused by the contraction of lower trunk muscles, releases about 300 to 400 million sperm from the body.

The Female Reproductive System   The main structures of the female reproductive system are located inside the body (see illustration: Female Reproductive System). The ovaries, fallopian tubes, uterus, and vagina are the major internal parts. External structures include two pairs of skin folds (*labia majora* and *labia minora*) and, behind these folds, the *clitoris,* an organ of sexual arousal.

Egg cells, or ova, are produced in the *ovaries,* a pair of organs connected by the *fallopian tubes* to the uterus. It is in the fallopian tubes that fertilization takes place. The *uterus* is a pear-shaped organ in which the egg, if fertilized by a sperm, develops into a *fetus*. A narrow opening in the uterus, called the *cervix,* leads to the *vagina*. The vagina provides an entrance for the penis during intercourse and an exit for a baby at birth.

Female Reproductive System.

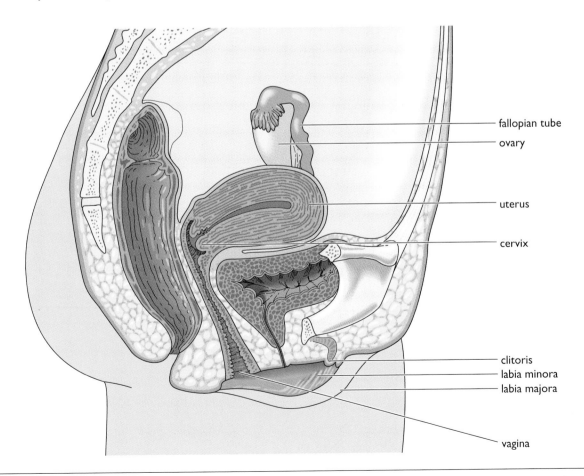

fallopian tube

ovary

uterus

cervix

clitoris
labia minora
labia majora

vagina

The Role of Menstruation   In females, hormones closely control a cycle that causes *menstruation,* which is bleeding from the uterus that takes place approximately every 28 days. As the ovaries prepare to release an egg, hormones signal the buildup of a lining in the uterus to prepare it to receive a fertilized egg. If the egg is not fertilized, the lining of the uterus is shed during the menstrual period. Menstruation begins at puberty and continues until a woman reaches menopause, usually in her mid-forties. *Menopause* signals the end of a woman's ability to conceive a child. (See also FEMALE REPRODUCTIVE SYSTEM, **6**; MALE REPRODUCTIVE SYSTEM, **6**; MENSTRUATION, **6**.)

▶ **RESPIRATORY SYSTEM**   The respiratory system processes the air you breathe. Its most important function is to provide oxygen to the blood and remove carbon dioxide from it. The respiratory system is closely linked to the CIRCULATORY SYSTEM, which acts as a transportation network for the oxygen and carbon dioxide.

The Structure and Function of the Respiratory System   You breathe air through your NOSE and MOUTH (see illustration: The Respiratory System). The air is moistened and warmed and impurities are trapped in the hairs and mucus that line the inside of the nose and sinuses. The SINUSES are air-filled cavities located in the bones surrounding the nose. Next, air enters the upper part of the throat and passes through the *larynx* (voice box). When you talk, it is the air that you breathe that vibrates the vocal cords, making sounds that you form into words with your mouth.

The *trachea* (windpipe) is the next step in the passage of air to the lungs. The trachea, a flexible tube about 1 inch (about 3 cm) in diameter and about 5 inches (about 13 cm) long, is lined with tiny moving hairs called *cilia.* The waving movement of cilia catches dust particles and other impurities and passes them upward and away from the lungs. The trachea divides into two branches called bronchial tubes that lead to the LUNGS. Within the lungs, the bronchial tubes further subdivide into *bronchi* (sing. *bronchus*) and *bronchioles.* Each bronchiole ends in a tiny group of bubblelike sacs called *alveoli* (sing. *alveolus*).

The Breathing Cycle   When you inhale, your DIAPHRAGM contracts, pushing down, and your rib cage lifts up and out. This makes more room for the air that is being drawn into the lungs. When you exhale, your diaphragm relaxes and your rib cage moves back to its original position. This compresses the chest cavity and gently forces the air up through the upper airway and out through the mouth and nose. An adult at rest inhales approximately 1 pint (about 0.5 L) of air 13 to 17 times per minute. In a normal day, you inhale and exhale more than 20,000 times.

> An adult at rest inhales approximately 1 pint (about 0.5 L) of air 13 to 17 times per minute. In a normal day, you inhale and exhale more than 20,000 times.

Respiration and Circulation   The lungs contain millions of the bubblelike sacs called alveoli. It is in the alveoli that the exchange of oxygen and carbon dioxide takes place. Microscopic blood vessels wind through the alveoli. These blood vessels filter the carbon dioxide out of the blood and replace it with oxygen. After the blood has been oxygenated, it flows through progressively larger veins until it reaches the pulmonary veins,

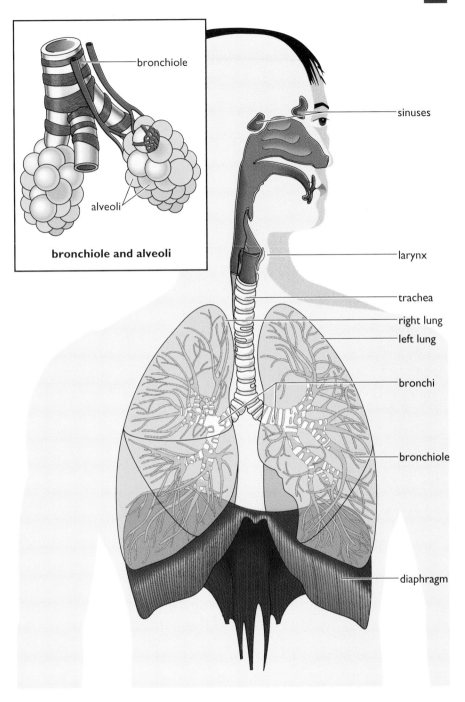

bronchiole

alveoli

bronchiole and alveoli

sinuses

larynx

trachea

right lung

left lung

bronchi

bronchiole

diaphragm

The Respiratory System.

which send the blood back to the heart. The heart pumps the blood through the circulatory system to deliver oxygen to the cells of your body and thus repeats the cycle.

Common Respiratory Problems   Diseases of the respiratory system occur when bacteria, viruses, and other foreign substances get past the system's defenses. The most common respiratory problems, both caused by viruses, are the *common cold* and *influenza*.

RISK FACTORS
▶ ▶ ▶ ▶ ▶ ▶

Prolonged exposure to cigarette smoke or air pollution can also lead to serious disease. Such substances actually damage the lungs and increase the possibility that a person will develop *bronchitis, emphysema,* or *lung cancer.* Cigarette smoking is believed to be a factor in more than 80 percent of all lung cancer cases.

How to Prevent Problems   The best thing that you can do for your respiratory system is to avoid exposure to cigarette smoke. Avoiding air pollutants and getting regular exercise will also help your system stay healthy. (See also COMMON COLD, **2**; ASTHMA, **3**.)

HEALTHY CHOICES
●●●●●●●●●●●●●

▶ SALIVARY GLAND

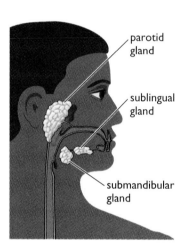

parotid
gland

sublingual
gland

submandibular
gland

Location of the Salivary Glands.   *The salivary glands are scattered throughout the interior of the mouth, ensuring that each bite of food is thoroughly moistened with saliva, so that you can swallow it. The saliva also helps wash away the food particles and bacteria present in the mouth after eating.*

Salivary glands secrete *saliva,* a thin, watery fluid, into the MOUTH through ducts. There are three main pairs of salivary glands (see illustration: Location of the Salivary Glands). The *parotid glands* are located in front of and below the ears, and the ducts of the parotid glands open into the cheeks. The *submandibular glands* are in the rear of the mouth on the floor, next to the jaws. The *sublingual glands* are in the front of the mouth on the floor, under the tongue. The submandibular ducts and the sublingual ducts both open under the tongue.

Saliva performs several important functions. It lubricates the interior of the mouth and throat. It also helps keep the mouth healthy because it contains antibodies that can kill bacteria. An enzyme in saliva begins the process of digesting carbohydrates. Saliva also moistens food, making it easier to chew and swallow. And finally, saliva enables you to taste the food you eat: The taste buds can detect flavors in food only after the food is moistened with saliva.

The salivary glands produce about 2 pints (1 L) of saliva per day. The sight, smell, taste, or thought of food can trigger the glands to produce saliva. In contrast, when you become dehydrated, your salivary glands reduce or stop the production of saliva. Your mouth then feels dry, signaling the brain that you are thirsty. A dry mouth can also result from taking certain medications, such as decongestants.

Common Salivary Gland Problems   The most common disorder of the salivary glands is *mumps,* a viral infection that causes the glands to become swollen. Bacterial infections can also invade the glands, causing abscesses. Small stones can form in the ducts or glands, causing pain and blockage. The stones, or at times the entire gland, can be removed surgically. *Sarcoidosis* is a rare swelling of unknown cause that can affect the salivary glands as well as other parts of the body.

Although saliva helps wash away bacteria and food particles in the mouth, it is still important to practice good oral hygiene to avoid tooth decay and infections of the mouth and salivary glands. (See also GLAND; MUMPS, **2**.)

HEALTHY CHOICES
●●●●●●●●●●●●●

▶ SCARRING

Scarring is a process that takes place when tough, fibrous TISSUE grows in place of tissue that has been damaged by a cut, burn, or surgical incision. Scars are a by-product of the healing process. Scar tissue is made up largely of *collagen,* a tough protein that is also a part of normal SKIN tissue. The purpose of scar tissue is to help the damaged tissue reform and hold together. Because scar tissue does not contain as many blood vessels and cells as normal tissue, it can restrict the movement or function of the healed tissue.

A *keloid scar* is a thick, raised, red mass of scar tissue that continues to grow after the wound has healed. A *hypertrophic scar* is a large scar that grows over a wound that has been infected. Large scars on the skin can be unsightly or disfiguring. Scars on internal organs are called *adhesions*. These are long strips of scar tissue that usually result from surgical procedures. Large adhesions can interfere with intestinal function and cause blockage.

A large cut or wound requires medical attention. The edges of the wound will be drawn together and stitched or taped in place to minimize scarring. (When the edges of a wound are close together, little scar tissue needs to form. This is why small wounds rarely leave noticeable scars.) New techniques and medications can also greatly reduce the scarring that occurs at the sites of serious burns. Plastic surgeons can usually remove unsightly scars and greatly improve a patient's appearance.

▶ ## SHOULDER

The shoulder is the JOINT where the upper arm meets the trunk of the body. It is a complex *ball-and-socket joint* that allows the arm to perform a wide range of movements. Strong muscles attached to the bones of the shoulder and arms provide the upper body strength needed to lift heavy objects.

The three bones that make up the shoulder are the long, narrow *clavicle* (collarbone), the triangular *scapula* (shoulder blade), and the *humerus*, the bone of the upper arm (see illustration: Bones of the Shoulder). The clavicle connects the scapula to the sternum (breastbone).

Bones of the Shoulder. *The clavicle (collarbone) connects the scapula (shoulder blade) to the sternum (breastbone). The scapula forms the socket, and the end of the humerus forms the ball of the ball-and-socket joint of the shoulder.*

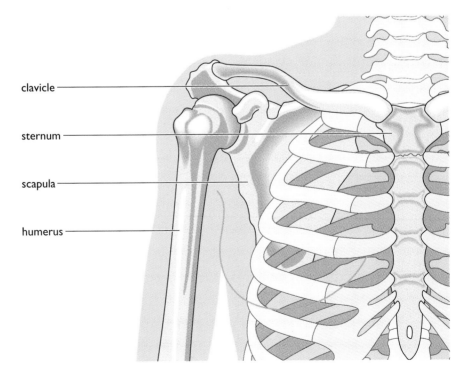

clavicle

sternum

scapula

humerus

The scapula forms the socket of the ball-and-socket joint of the shoulder. The end of the humerus forms the ball. The joint is surrounded by a strong membrane of fibrous tissue called the *synovium,* which secretes a fluid that lubricates the joint. A fluid-filled sac, the *bursa,* is located under the bony tip of the shoulder blade. The bursa cushions the socket and reduces friction among the three shoulder bones as they move against one another. Many strong *ligaments* and three sets of powerful MUSCLES— the deltoid, trapezius, and latissimus dorsi—control the movements of the shoulder and hold the parts of the joint in place.

Common Shoulder Problems Because the clavicle is so thin and narrow, it is easily broken. A dislocated shoulder is another common injury. When the shoulder is dislocated, the humerus is displaced from its normal position in the socket. Dislocation is usually caused by a sharp forward or backward blow to the shoulder. Treatment for a dislocated shoulder includes placing the humerus back in the socket and holding it in place with a sling for several weeks. Repeated dislocations may require surgery to tighten damaged muscles and ligaments. The shoulder joint is also susceptible to *bursitis,* an inflammation of the bursa, and to "frozen shoulder," an inflammation of the joint capsule that causes pain and stiffness. Degenerative joint diseases, such as osteoarthritis and rheumatoid arthritis, can also affect the shoulder joint. (See also BURSITIS, **3.**)

SINUS

The sinuses are air-filled cavities located in the bones surrounding the nose. You have eight sinuses; each is lined with membrane that secretes *mucus,* a thick, slippery substance that drains into the nose and throat. When air is inhaled, it passes through the nose and sinuses, where it is warmed and moistened with mucus, before it is transported to the lungs. Because the sinuses are hollow, they serve as resonating chambers that determine the pitch or tone of one's voice. The sinus cavities also lighten the skull, making it easier to hold up the head.

The eight sinuses are divided into four pairs. The frontal sinuses are located in the frontal bone just above the eyebrows. The sphenoid sinuses lie between the eyes deeper in the skull. The ethmoid sinuses are positioned on each side of the nose between the nose and each eye

The Sinuses.

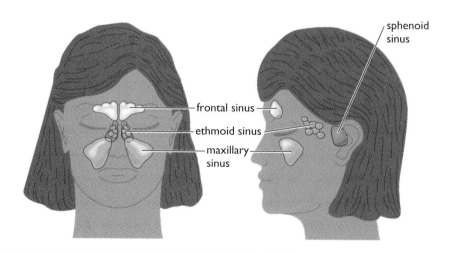

socket. The maxillary sinuses are large cavities in the cheeks on each side of the nose directly above the upper teeth (see illustration: The Sinuses).

Sinus Problems *Sinusitis* is an inflammation of the MUCOUS MEMBRANES of the sinuses. Symptoms may include headache, fever, and difficulty in breathing. Sinusitis is often caused by a bacterial infection carried by mucus from the nose to the sinuses. Colds, allergies, or a diseased tooth can trigger sinusitis. Acute sinusitis usually occurs after a cold and may last for a week to 10 days. Chronic or long-term sinusitis occurs when repeated infections have narrowed or closed off the opening of the sinus so it cannot drain. A *deviated septum,* a misalignment of the partition in the nose, can also cause chronic sinusitis by blocking the sinus opening. Physicians usually treat sinusitis by prescribing decongestants and antibiotics. In some severe cases, surgery may be necessary to drain the sinuses. (See also SINUSITIS, **2.**)

▶ **SKELETON**   **see MUSCULOSKELETAL SYSTEM**

▶ **SKIN**

> The skin is the largest and one of the most complex organs of the body. It covers the body and protects the other organs and systems.

The skin is the largest and one of the most complex organs of the body. It performs several important functions. It covers the body and protects the other organs and systems from injuries, infections, and the effects of sunlight. It helps regulate body temperature, waterproofs the body, and determines a person's appearance. The skin is also a major sensory organ that is sensitive to touch, pressure, pain, and temperature. The average person's body is covered by about 17 square feet (about 1.6 sq m) of skin, yet most of the skin is only about $1/10$ inch (about 2.5 mm) thick.

Structure of the Skin The skin consists of three layers: the epidermis, the dermis, and the subcutaneous layer (see illustration: Skin Structure). The top layer, the *epidermis,* is made up of several bands of flat, cube-shaped cells. At the bottom of the epidermis are the *basal cells;* these divide into new cells that are constantly pushing older cells up toward the surface of the skin. As the older cells rise, they die and are sloughed off to make room for the newer cells. The epidermis also contains cells that produce *melanin,* a brown pigment that protects the skin from sunlight and determines skin color.

Below the epidermis is the *dermis,* flexible connective tissue made up largely of various fibers and water. Interspersed throughout the dermis are blood vessels, sweat glands, nerve cells, and hair follicles. Both the blood vessels and the sweat glands regulate body temperature. Blood vessels expand to get rid of heat (causing flushed skin) and tighten to conserve heat (causing pallor). The evaporation of sweat from skin cools the skin's surface. The nerve cells respond to touch, pressure, and temperature. Oil-secreting *sebaceous glands* attached to the hair follicles lubricate the skin and hair. The third layer of the skin is the *subcutaneous*

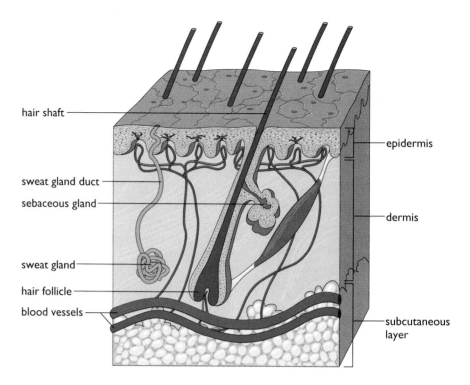

hair shaft

sweat gland duct

sebaceous gland

sweat gland

hair follicle

blood vessels

epidermis

dermis

subcutaneous layer

Skin Structure.

layer, which is made up largely of fat cells. This layer insulates the body, and its fat cells provide a reserve source of energy.

Skin Problems   There are numerous disorders and diseases of the skin. Most are not life-threatening but can be irritating or disabling. *Acne* is an inflammation and blockage of the sebaceous glands of the hair follicles. *Chicken pox* and *warts* are viral infections of the skin, while *boils* and *impetigo* are caused by bacteria. Fungi cause *athlete's foot* and ringworm. Allergies can also affect the skin. *Hives* are an allergic reaction to certain substances. Aging can have a number of negative effects on the skin, including discolorations known as liver (or age) spots and dryness, wrinkling, or leathery toughening of the skin.

The skin is subject to many common injuries such as cuts, bites, and burns. Severe burns over a large portion of the body can cause death. Prolonged exposure to sunlight causes the skin to dry and age prematurely. Sun damage is the most common cause of *skin cancer.* Most skin cancers can be cured easily if they are detected early. But malignant melanoma, which often starts with molelike growths, can spread rapidly to other parts of the body and cause disfigurement and even death. Treatment in the early stages, however, is usually successful. (See also SKIN CANCER, 3.)

HEALTHY CHOICES

CONSULT A
PHYSICIAN

Skin Care   Keep your skin clean and dry to avoid bacterial and fungal infections. Use a moisturizer on dry skin to prevent premature aging, and use only mild soaps. If you have severe acne, consult a *dermatologist,* a physician who specializes in skin problems. Finally, when you spend time in the sun, use sun screens, which absorb ultraviolet rays, and sun blockers, which deflect the rays. Wear sunglasses, a hat, and other protective clothing. (See also NAIL; SCARRING; ITCHING, 2; RASH, 2; ACNE, 3; SUNSCREENS, 8; PHYSICIANS (M.D.'s)—DERMATOLOGIST, 9.)

► SKULL

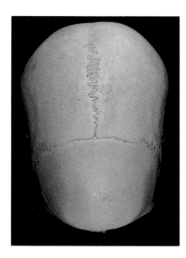

Suture Joints of the Skull. *At birth, the skull bones are soft at the joints. The hard, zigzag suture joints form during the first few years of life.*

The skull is the bony framework of the head. It surrounds and protects the BRAIN and houses four of the five sense organs: the ears, eyes, nose, and tongue. The skull is made up of 22 bones. Most of these bones are fused to form one rigid structure that protects the skull's delicate contents. The JAW, however, is not fused. It meets the skull at the temporomandibular joint, a powerful *hinge joint* that enables the mouth to chew and grind food.

Structure of the Skull   The bones of the skull are divided into two groups: the 8 cranial bones that encase the brain and the 14 facial bones that form the structure of the face and mouth. In infants, the cranial bones are not fused, but they gradually grow together, meeting at immovable joints called *sutures* (see illustration: Suture Joints of the Skull).

The skull has several cavities, or hollows. The largest cavity, the cranial cavity, houses the brain. The nasal cavity lies behind the nose, and two other cavities called orbits form the eye sockets. There are also cavities for the ears. In addition to these openings at the nose, eyes, and ears, there is an opening in the base of the skull through which the spinal cord descends to the torso.

Skull Injuries and Disorders   A blow to the head may cause the skull bone to crack. A simple crack usually heals on its own. However, a serious skull injury, in which bone fragments are displaced, can cause brain damage. This damage can be caused by skull fragments or by pressure on the brain from bleeding, called a hemorrhage, in the tissues that cover the brain. In such cases surgery may be needed to remove bone fragments from the surface of the brain and to repair broken blood vessels. You should protect your skull against injury by wearing a helmet when cycling, skating, or participating in contact sports such as football and hockey.

Sometimes a baby is born with a *cleft palate,* a common defect in which the bony structures at the roof of the mouth fail to grow together before birth. A cleft palate can cause difficulties eating and speaking, but in most cases it can be surgically corrected soon after birth. (See also MUSCULOSKELETAL SYSTEM.)

► SLEEP

Sleep is a period of unconsciousness during which the brain and the body rest. Humans spend about one-third of their lives sleeping. No one knows why sleep is necessary, but scientists believe that it reenergizes the body and enables the nervous system to dispose of waste products built up during wakefulness. They also think that the dreams that occur during sleep give the brain a chance to deal with information it has gathered during the day. When people are deprived of sleep, they become irritable, fatigued, and unable to carry out routine tasks. After several days of sleep deprivation, people become disoriented and begin to hallucinate.

Stages of Sleep   Experiments have shown that people experience two distinct types of sleep (see illustration: Stages of Sleep). When they first fall asleep, their breathing and heart rate slow and their brains generate deep, slow *delta waves.* This is called slow-wave or non-REM sleep.

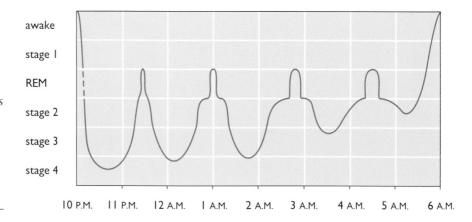

Stages of Sleep. *A person passes through successive stages of sleep during the night in cycles of about 90 minutes. The pattern begins with non-REM sleep, (stages 1, 2, 3, and 4), followed by a brief period of REM sleep. As the night wears on, the periods of REM sleep grow longer.*

After about an hour and a half, the sleeper enters the REM stage of sleep. *REM* and *non-REM* refer to the term *rapid eye movement*. In REM sleep, which lasts from 5 to 20 minutes at a time, the eyes move back and forth rapidly under the closed lids. (In non-REM sleep, these movements do not occur.) Also in REM sleep, the brain gives off *beta waves* that are similar to the brain waves people register when they are awake. It is during this stage of sleep that dreaming takes place. Throughout the course of one night's sleep, the sleeper alternates between REM and non-REM sleep at about 90-minute intervals.

Sleep Disorders Most adults need 7 to 9 hours of sleep every night, although some need more and others can do with much less. Children typically need a few more hours' sleep than adults. People who have trouble falling asleep or staying asleep are suffering from *insomnia*. When people are anxious or excited, they may have trouble falling asleep for a few days or even weeks. Some people can fall asleep easily but have trouble staying asleep. *Sleep apnea* is a condition in which a person's breathing stops for brief periods during sleep. People who suffer from *narcolepsy* fall asleep suddenly at inappropriate times during the day. Many people occasionally have trouble maintaining a regular sleep schedule. When people travel across several time zones, they often suffer a disruption of their sleep schedule called jet lag, which lasts a few days until their "internal clocks" can adjust to the new schedule.

Getting a Good Night's Sleep There are several things you can do to get a good night's sleep. Exercise during the day—but not just before bedtime—to make yourself physically tired. Take a warm bath to relax or drink a glass of warm milk. Milk contains a substance that promotes relaxation. If you still cannot sleep, get up and stay up until you feel sleepy. No matter how little sleep you manage to get, arise at your normal time the next morning and avoid napping during the day to help your body get back to its normal schedule.

People who have trouble sleeping should not take medication such as sleeping pills for more than a few days at a time because they may become dependent on the pills. Sleep disorders are often a symptom of other underlying illnesses or problems. If they persist, the sufferer should consult a physician. A few hospitals have sleep disorder clinics where people with chronic sleep problems can seek help. (See also SLEEP DISORDERS, 3; DREAMS, 5; SLEEP PROBLEMS, 5.)

CONSULT A
PHYSICIAN

▶ SPINAL CORD

The spinal cord is a tapered column of nerve tissue that extends from the BRAIN and descends down the back. The spinal cord's primary function is to transmit sensory and motor information to and from the brain along the body's extensive network of NEURONS (nerve cells). The spinal cord also controls the involuntary REFLEX ACTION of the muscles, which causes you to move away or protect yourself from pain or danger.

Structure of the Spinal Cord   The spinal cord is about as thick as a finger and about 17 or 18 inches (43 to 46 cm) long. A column of gray matter is at the center of the spinal cord. It contains the cell bodies of motor and connecting neurons. Through the cell bodies, which are the neurons' relay centers, motor neurons send messages to muscles and glands. Connecting neurons send messages to other neurons within the spinal cord and brain. The gray matter also contains the nerve fibers (axons) of sensory neurons. (The cell bodies of these neurons lie outside the gray matter.) These axons connect with the motor and connecting neurons.

The gray matter is surrounded by an oval disk of white matter. The white matter consists of bundles of sensory and motor nerve fibers that are coated with a protective material called *myelin*. These fibers extend along the length of the spinal cord. An ascending tract carries information to the brain, and a descending tract carries messages from the brain.

At regular points on either side of the cord, bundles of nerve fibers emerge. These bundles form spinal nerves. In all, 31 pairs of spinal nerves carry information between the spinal cord and the rest of the body.

The bones, or *vertebrae* (sing. *vertebra*), of the spinal column protect the spinal cord. In addition, the cord is covered and protected by three layers of membranes called the *spinal meninges*. The area between the middle and inner membranes is filled with cerebrospinal fluid that helps to absorb shocks to the spinal cord.

Disorders of the Spinal Cord   The most common disorder of the spinal cord is spinal cord injury. If the spinal cord is severed, all the nerves below the point of injury cease to function, causing paralysis. A severed spinal cord cannot be repaired because the nerves of the cord will not grow back together. Multiple sclerosis is a disease of the spinal cord caused by inflammation of the myelin sheath. Meningitis is a rare but serious infection of the meninges surrounding the spinal cord.

Cross Section of the Spinal Cord.

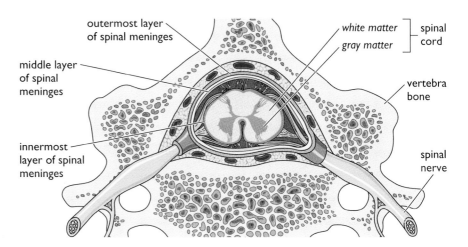

outermost layer of spinal meninges

middle layer of spinal meninges

innermost layer of spinal meninges

white matter

gray matter

} spinal cord

vertebra bone

spinal nerve

Preventing Spinal Cord Injuries Spinal cord injuries occur most commonly as a result of automobile accidents, gunshot wounds, and diving accidents. To avoid a spinal cord injury, always wear a seat belt in a car, and never drink alcohol and drive. When diving into a body of water, follow this rule: If the water does not cover your head when you stand in it, it is too shallow to dive into. Also, never dive into water without making sure it is clear of obstacles. (See also NERVOUS SYSTEM.)

HEALTHY CHOICES
●●●●●●●●●●●●

▶ SPINE

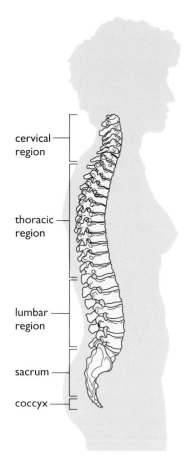

cervical region

thoracic region

lumbar region

sacrum

coccyx

Regions of the Spine. *The top of the spine—the cervical region—is made up of 7 vertebrae. The next 12 vertebrae make up the thoracic region. The lumbar region, in the lower back, consists of 5 vertebrae. The sacrum, consisting of 5 fused vertebrae, forms part of the pelvis. The spine ends at the coccyx, or tailbone, which consists of 4 fused vertebrae.*

The spine is the long column of knobby bones that runs down the back from the base of the skull to the pelvis. It supports and balances the head and the trunk, enabling a person to stand upright. In addition, the bones of the spine surround and protect the SPINAL CORD, the thick column of nerve fibers that carry messages to and from the brain and all parts of the body.

The Structure of the Spine The spine is made up of 33 bones, or *vertebrae* (sing. *vertebra*). The vertebrae are divided into five regions (see illustration: Regions of the Spine). Each vertebra is a hollow cylinder with three short spurs that project outward, one to each side and one to the back. The spurs are the points where the back muscles attach to the spine. The hollow centers of the vertebrae house the spinal cord. Each vertebra is connected to the vertebrae above and below it. The connecting joints are cushioned by *disks*, or pads, of tough, fibrous cartilage. The disks are filled with a jellylike tissue that enables them to absorb the jars and shocks to the spine caused by walking and other movements. There are openings between the vertebrae, and nerves branch off from the spinal cord through these openings to all parts of the body.

The spine does not form a straight line; rather, it curves in four places, like an elongated S. These curves are believed to absorb shocks and increase the flexibility of the spine.

Spinal Problems Any injury to the back can be serious because of the possibility of damaging the spinal cord. Severe damage to the spinal cord can result in paralysis or death. Most spinal injuries are caused by automobile accidents, gunshot wounds, and diving accidents. The victim of a spinal cord or back injury should not be moved except by a physician or trained rescue workers. The wrong movement could cause further damage.

One of the most common disorders of the spine is a *herniated disk,* which occurs when the capsule surrounding a disk bulges, pushing against a spinal nerve. This condition can be painful, but it can be corrected surgically. *Scoliosis* is an abnormal curving of the spine to the right or left. When detected early, it can be corrected by physical therapy or by wearing a spinal brace.

Back pain is typically caused by overstressing the back muscles. Many people suffer from pain in the lower back (lumbar) region. You can avoid injuries to your back muscles by using your leg muscles to help lift heavy weights. You can further protect your spine and back by sitting up straight and by sleeping on a firm mattress. (See also MUSCULOSKELETAL SYSTEM; BACK PROBLEMS, 3; SCOLIOSIS, 3.)

▶ ## STOMACH   see DIGESTIVE SYSTEM

▶ ## TENDON   see CONNECTIVE TISSUE

▶ ## THROAT

The throat (pharynx) is the passageway inside the neck that connects the nose and mouth with the trachea (windpipe) and esophagus. The throat also contains the *larynx* (voicebox) where you produce the sounds needed for speech.

The throat plays a key role in both the RESPIRATORY SYSTEM and the DIGESTIVE SYSTEM. When you breathe, air travels through your throat and larynx and into your trachea and lungs. When you eat or drink, the muscles in your throat push the food into your esophagus, which carries it to your stomach. Both food and air travel through the main part of the throat. The *epiglottis,* a flap of cartilage at the top of the larynx, closes off the trachea

The Throat. *One of the primary functions of the throat is swallowing. Swallowing a bite of food involves precise coordination of the actions of the mouth, tongue, throat, larynx, and esophagus. If this process fails in some way, food can become lodged in the lower part of the throat.*

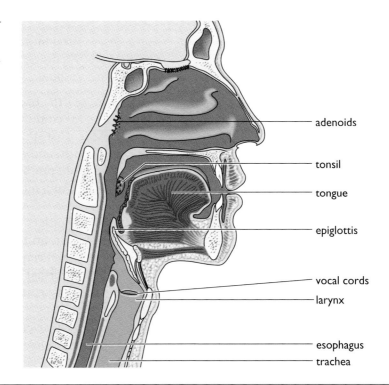

- adenoids
- tonsil
- tongue
- epiglottis
- vocal cords
- larynx
- esophagus
- trachea

during swallowing. This prevents food from entering the breathing passage, which would cause choking (see illustration: The Throat).

The Structure of the Throat   The main part of the throat is a muscular tube ringed with cartilage and lined with MUCOUS MEMBRANE (this lubricates and protects the throat). At the upper end of the throat is a channel to the nasal passages and an opening to the mouth; at the lower end are two tubes, the trachea and the esophagus. The larynx is located at the entrance to the trachea.

The throat also contains the TONSILS, two tissue masses at the back of the mouth that trap germs before they enter the throat and cause infection. Similar tissue masses called ADENOIDS are located at the back of nasal passages; they, too, help fight infection as part of the body's IMMUNE SYSTEM.

The Larynx and Vocal Cords   The larynx is made up of nine cartilages and includes the *vocal cords*, two elastic sheets of tissue that produce the voice. The vocal cords stretch from the large thyroid cartilage (which forms the *Adam's apple*) in the front of the larynx to two movable cartilages at the rear. When the vocal cords are at rest, they form a V-shaped opening (called the *glottis*) through which air passes during ordinary breathing. In order to produce sound, muscles pull the vocal cords together, and air exhaled from the lungs makes them vibrate. The closer they are drawn together, the higher the tone of the sounds produced. The tongue and lips give shape to the sounds to create speech.

Common Throat Problems   *Pharyngitis,* commonly known as *sore throat,* is an often painful inflammation of the throat. Viral infections (such as colds or chicken pox), bacterial infections (such as strep throat), tobacco smoke, and pollutants can cause pharyngitis. The usual cure for most sore throats is rest and pain relievers; antibiotics are used to treat bacterial throat infections. Persistent or severe sore throats should be investigated by a physician.

CONSULT A
PHYSICIAN

Laryngitis, an inflammation of the larynx, can cause hoarseness or temporary loss of the voice. It may be caused by a cold or by overstraining the vocal cords. Allergies, pollutants, or overuse of the voice can produce *polyps,* small swellings on the vocal cords that may change the voice. The usual treatment for polyps is rest and voice therapy to retrain the vocal cords. Sometimes, however, surgery may be necessary to remove the growths. If any hoarseness does not clear up after a week, a physician should examine the larynx. Persistent hoarseness may be a symptom of cancer of the larynx.

Bones or large pieces of food can become trapped in the throat, causing choking. You should learn the *Heimlich maneuver* to help anyone who appears to be choking. (See also LARYNGITIS, **2**; SORE THROAT, **2**; HEIMLICH MANEUVER, **8**.)

▶ # THYROID GLAND   The thyroid gland is a large gland located at the base of the neck just below the *larynx* (see illustration: Location of the Thyroid Gland). The largest gland of the ENDOCRINE SYSTEM, it produces two hormones that

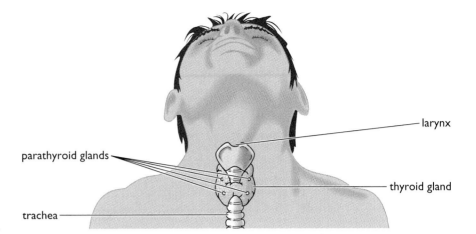

Location of the Thyroid Gland.
The thyroid gland consists of two lobes that surround the trachea (windpipe).

are essential for normal growth and development. It also produces a hormone that controls the amount of calcium in the blood. These hormones are released directly into the bloodstream, which transports them throughout the body.

The two main hormones produced by the thyroid gland are *thyroxine* (T$_4$) and *triiodothyronine* (T$_3$). These hormones play an important role in controlling the body's METABOLISM, which is the rate at which cells convert nutrients to energy. In children, T$_3$ and T$_4$ are also important for ensuring normal growth and development.

The third hormone produced by the thyroid gland, *calcitonin,* helps to regulate the amount of calcium in the blood. When the calcium level is too high, the thyroid gland releases calcitonin into the bloodstream. The calcitonin stimulates the circulatory system to deposit the excess calcium in the bones and teeth. When the calcium level is too low, the thyroid suppresses production of calcitonin so that the calcium level can rise back to normal.

The Parathyroids   Calcitonin works in conjunction with hormones produced by the parathyroid glands. The four parathyroid glands are located next to the thyroid gland. These glands release parathyroid hormone, which increases the amounts of calcium in the blood. The correct levels of calcium are essential to healthy bones, normal nerve and muscle function, cell-membrane function, and blood clotting.

Disorders of the Thyroid Gland   Normally, the thyroid gland produces just enough hormones to keep the metabolic rate in balance. *Hyperthyroidism* is a disease that occurs when the thyroid overproduces hormones. Symptoms include anxiety, sweating, weight loss, and sensitivity to heat. *Hypothyroidism* is the underproduction of thyroid hormones. Its symptoms include fatigue, weight gain, dry skin, and sensitivity to cold. Hypothyroidism in childhood causes *cretinism,* mental retardation and stunted growth. These imbalances can usually be corrected by taking synthetic hormones.

Goiter is an enlargement of the thyroid gland caused by the absence of iodine from the diet. It has become rare in the United States because most people use iodized table salt or eat fish that contain high levels of iodine. (See also THYROID DISORDERS, **3.**)

▷ TISSUE

Tissue is a group of cells that perform the same kind of function. Some types of tissue protect the body; others enable it to move. Still other tissues absorb, secrete, and transport substances essential to body functions. Groups of different tissues form organs.

Tissue includes both the CELLS, the living portion of the tissue, and the fluid and nonliving substances surrounding the cells. The fluid, called *interstitial* fluid, carries oxygen, hormones, and nutrients to the cells from the bloodstream. It also carries waste material from the cells back to the bloodstream. A disturbance in the balance of fluid in the tissues can cause *edema,* a swelling of the tissues. This sometimes occurs during pregnancy or when a person's heart is not functioning correctly.

Types of Tissue   There are four main types of tissue in the human body.

- *Epithelial tissue* makes up the SKIN and the linings of the internal organs. It protects the body from microorganisms and absorbs nutrients from digested food.
- The MUSCLES are made up of *muscle tissue,* groups of elastic cells that contract.
- CONNECTIVE TISSUE joins or supports parts of the body. For example, tendons and ligaments connect muscles and bones so that the muscles can move the skeleton. Other connective tissues support internal organs.
- *Nerve tissue* receives information from the sense organs and transports messages from the brain to various parts of the body.

▷ TONGUE   see MOUTH

▷ TONSIL

Tonsils are two TISSUE masses located on either side of the THROAT at the base of the tongue. They are part of the LYMPHATIC SYSTEM, which plays an important role in your body's efforts to ward off infection. The tonsils fight infection by trapping microorganisms before they enter the throat and by producing antibodies. The tonsils normally stop performing these functions by about age 3 and gradually grow smaller as a person matures.

Tonsillitis is an inflammation of the tonsils that occurs when bacteria overwhelm the tonsils. In some children, the tonsils are repeatedly infected and become enlarged. If a child suffers several attacks of tonsillitis, or if the tonsils become so large that they obstruct the passageways of the throat, a physician may surgically remove the tonsils. This operation, called a tonsillectomy, used to be performed routinely on children. Since the discovery of antibiotics, however, tonsillectomies are performed much less frequently. (See also IMMUNE SYSTEM; TONSILLITIS, **2.**)

► TOOTH

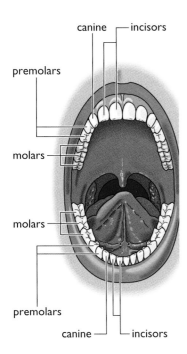

Adult Teeth.

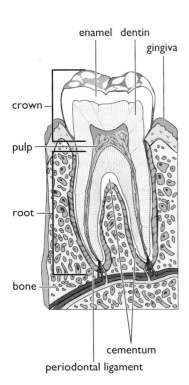

Parts of a Tooth.

Teeth perform the first step in the process of food digestion. The hard, bonelike surfaces of the teeth tear and grind each mouthful of food into small pieces that can be swallowed and digested. Along with the lips and tongue, the teeth help people form the sounds used in talking.

Tooth Development   Teeth begin to form under the gums in the fetus during the third or fourth month of pregnancy. They begin to cut through the gums 6 or 7 months after the baby is born. Two sets of teeth develop during a person's lifetime. Beginning at about 6 years of age, 20 primary, or deciduous, teeth are gradually replaced by 32 permanent teeth.

The teeth are specialized to perform three different jobs (see illustration: Adult Teeth). The 8 front teeth, the *incisors,* are shovel-shaped, with a sharp cutting edge for biting off pieces of food. The 4 *canines* (cuspids) are sharp and pointed for tearing food fibers. The 8 *premolars* (bicuspids) and 12 *molars* in the back of the mouth have broad, flattened surfaces for grinding and chewing food into small bits.

Tooth Structure   Each tooth is covered with a hard, insensitive coating of *enamel,* the hardest substance in the body (see illustration: Parts of a Tooth). Under the enamel is the *dentin,* a hard, dense material that can feel pressure and temperature. Most of the tooth consists of dentin, which is made up of cells arranged in rows of tubules, or tiny canals. The dentin covers the *pulp,* where the nerves and blood vessels that nourish the tooth are found. The pulp is sensitive to pain, pressure, and temperature.

The visible portion of the tooth is called the *crown.* Each tooth is surrounded by the *gums,* or gingivae, the soft tissue covering the jawbones. The portion of the tooth below the gumline is the *root,* where the nerves and blood vessels enter a tooth. The root is covered and protected by another hard substance, the *cementum.* Teeth fit into sockets in the jawbone and are anchored to the bone by the *periodontal ligament,* a strong connective tissue that adheres to the cementum and the jawbone.

Disorders of the Teeth   Tooth decay, or *caries,* is one of the most common diseases to afflict humans. It occurs when acid, formed by food particles and bacteria, eats away the enamel, forming a cavity. Bacteria then invade the dentin and pulp and eventually kill the nerve. An abscessed tooth is one in which the invading bacteria inflame the surrounding tissue and generate pus. *Periodontitis* is inflammation of the supporting structures of the tooth. It occurs when plaque, a sticky deposit of food and bacteria, forms between the tooth and the gum. Inflammation of the gums, *gingivitis,* is an early symptom of periodontitis. Misaligned teeth can be unsightly and cause problems such as blocking or displacing surrounding teeth. Many children wear braces for up to 2 years to realign the teeth. Braces may be uncomfortable, but they result in a straighter bite.

The most important step in tooth care is developing the habit of brushing the teeth at least twice a day with a toothpaste containing fluoride. *Flossing,* inserting a thread called floss between each of the teeth, is also important. Flossing helps dislodge plaque and food particles that the toothbrush can't reach and should be part of daily tooth care. Everyone should form the habit of seeing a dentist at least twice a year to have the teeth cleaned and to have tooth disorders treated at an early stage. (See also DENTAL EXAMINATION; JAW; MOUTH; DENTAL PROBLEMS, **3**; GUM DISEASE, **3**; ORTHODONTIC DEVICES, **3**; DENTAL CARE, **9**.)

▶ TRACHEA   see RESPIRATORY SYSTEM

▶ URINALYSIS

A urinalysis is a series of tests performed to analyze urine. Changes in its makeup can signal infection, imbalance, or underlying disease.

What Urinalysis Shows   A urinalysis tests for the presence of certain substances—substances that are not normally present in the urine of a healthy individual. For example, the presence of glucose, or sugar, in the urine may suggest diabetes. Blood in the urine may indicate infection, tumors, or kidney stones. Protein in the urine may be a sign of damage to the blood vessels supplying the kidneys or other kidney disease. Bile may signify liver disease. Crystals may indicate a problem with metabolism, possibility of kidney stones, or presence of worm eggs caused by a parasite. Urinalysis can also be used to test for the presence of drugs, especially illegal drugs.

The sediment of the urine sometimes contains red or white blood cells. Red blood cells may mean that there is kidney disease or problems with the urinary tract. White blood cells usually signal infection.

How a Urinalysis Is Done   A routine urinalysis requires the patient to urinate into a container, which is then sent to the lab or examined in the office. For some of the tests, a drop is put on a glass slide and is examined under a microscope. Other tests use specially treated sticks, which change color when dipped into the sample.

A *clean-catch specimen* is taken from midway through the urination. It is required if infection is suspected, because the first few ounces of urine may be contaminated by bacteria in the tube leading to the outside of the body.

A *timed specimen* is used to test for substances, such as hormones, that are excreted on an irregular schedule. The patient collects all urine during a 12- to 24-hour period and saves it in a special collection container.

Some tests require a urine sample from the first void of the day because the urine is more concentrated and may contain substances that will not show up later in the day. (See also LIVER; URINARY TRACT.)

▶ URINARY TRACT

The urinary tract consists of the kidneys, the bladder, and tubes known as the ureters and the urethra (see illustration: Parts of the Urinary Tract). These organs and tubes, along with a network of blood

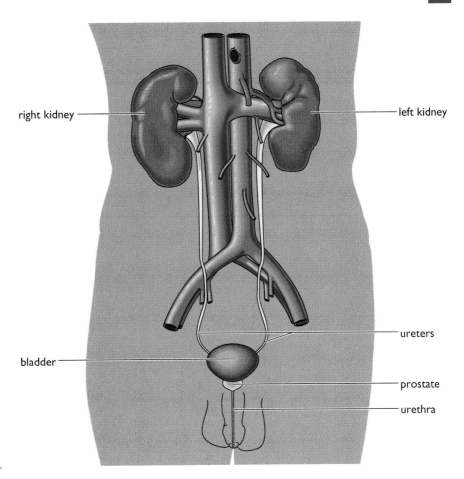

right kidney

left kidney

ureters

bladder

prostate

urethra

Parts of the Urinary Tract.
Blood is filtered in the kidneys and becomes urine. The urine then passes from the kidneys to the bladder via the ureters.

vessels, remove water and dissolved wastes from the blood and discharge them from the body as *urine*.

How the Urinary Tract Works   Blood entering the KIDNEYS travels from arteries into tiny clusters of capillaries. From these capillaries, it flows through the kidneys' filtering system, where wastes are separated and dissolved to become urine. Purified blood is returned to the veins, and urine travels out of the kidneys through the two *ureters*. Muscles in the walls of these tubes contract to push the urine along to the bladder. The *bladder* is a hollow, muscular holding sac for urine. Your bladder can store about 1 pint (about 0.5 L) of urine before you will feel the urge to urinate. At that point, a strong circular muscle at the bottom of the bladder is relaxed and allows the urine to flow into the *urethra,* the tube that carries the urine out of the body. In infants, the bladder empties automatically when it is full. By the age of 5, most children can control this impulse even when asleep.

Common Urinary Tract Problems   Occasionally, substances such as cholesterol build up in the kidney and form kidney stones. If these stones get stuck in the urinary tract, they may cause severe pain. Infections and difficulty in controlling the impulse to urinate often result from disorders in the urinary tract. You can help keep your urinary tract healthy by drinking plenty of liquids, especially water. (See also CYSTITIS, **2**; INCONTINENCE, **3**; KIDNEY DISORDERS, **3**.)

HEALTHY CHOICES
●●●●●●●●●●●●

▶ VEIN

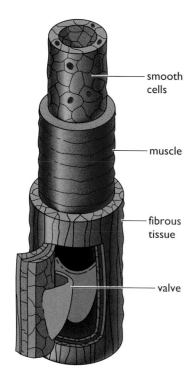

smooth cells

muscle

fibrous tissue

valve

Structure of a Vein. *Valves in the veins prevent the blood from flowing in the wrong direction.*

Veins are blood vessels or tubes in the CIRCULATORY SYSTEM that carry blood back to the heart from organs and tissues throughout the body. Most veins transport "blue" or oxygen-poor blood that is high in carbon dioxide. Pulmonary veins, however, carry oxygen-rich blood from the lungs to the heart.

Structure of the Veins Vein walls have layers of fibrous tissue, muscle, and smooth cells. Although these walls are not as thick as ARTERY walls, this does not present a problem because blood pressure in the veins is weaker than it is in the arteries. If blood pressure drops too low, however, veins will collapse.

Gentle pressure on the vein walls from surrounding muscles helps move the blood along. Valves in the veins control the direction of the movement. They allow blood to flow toward the heart but prevent it from flowing back away from the heart (see illustration: Structure of a Vein).

Vein Disorders *Varicose veins,* the most common vein problem, result from a backflow of blood caused by the force of gravity when, for instance, a person stands for long periods. Varicose veins are usually distended, swollen, and discolored. *Phlebitis* is a fairly common disorder marked by the inflammation of a vein. This may be caused by an injury or infection. (See also VARICOSE VEIN, 3.)

SUPPLEMENTARY SOURCES

Asimov, Isaac. 1963. *The human brain.* New York: Houghton Mifflin.

Bork, Joseph P. 1987. *Skin secrets: A complete guide to skin care for the entire family.* New York: McGraw-Hill.

Carskadon, Mary A., ed. 1993. *Encyclopedia of sleep and dreaming.* New York: Macmillan.

Clayman, Charles B., Jeffrey Kunz, and Harriet S. Meyer, eds. 1988. *The American Medical Association home medical adviser.* New York: Random House.

Dixon, Bernard, ed. 1986. *Health, medicine, and the human body.* New York: Macmillan.

Gonzales-Crussi, F. 1989. *The five senses.* New York: Harcourt.

Guinness, Alma E., ed. 1987. *ABC's of the human body: A family answer book.* Pleasantville, N.Y.: The Readers Digest Association.

McGowen, Tom. 1988. *The circulatory system: From Harvey to the artificial heart.* New York: Franklin Watts.

McGrew, Roderick E. 1985. *Encyclopedia of medical history.* New York: McGraw-Hill.

Omni's future medical almanac. 1987. New York: McGraw-Hill.

Silverstein, Alvin, and Virginia Silverstein. 1986. *World of the brain.* New York: William Morrow.

Squire, Larry R., ed. 1992. *Encyclopedia of learning and memory.* New York: Macmillan.

Taintor, Jerry F., and Mary Jane Taintor. 1988. *The oral report: The consumer's commonsense guide to better dental care.* New York: Facts on File.

Vickery, Donald M., and James Fries. 1986. *Take care of yourself: The consumer's guide to medical care.* 3d ed. Reading, Mass.: Addison-Wesley.

Walzer, Richard A. 1989. *Healthy skin: A guide to lifelong skin care.* Mt. Vernon, N.Y.: Consumers Union.

Ward, Brian R. 1988. *Dental care.* New York: Franklin Watts.

Weiss, Deborah L. 1986. *Eye care.* Springhouse, Pa.: Springhouse Corp.

Zinn, Walter J., and Herbert Solomon. 1986. *The complete guide to eye care, eyeglasses, and contact lenses,* rev. ed. Hollywood, Fla.: Frederick Fell.

ORGANIZATIONS

American Academy of Pediatrics
141 Northwest Point Boulevard
P.O. Box 927
Elk Grove Village, IL 60009
(708) 228-5005

American Association of Retired Persons
1909 K Street, NW
Washington, DC 20049
(202) 872-4700

American Dental Association
211 East Chicago Avenue
Chicago, IL 60611
(312) 440-2500

American Medical Association
515 North State Street
Chicago, IL 60610
(312) 464-5000

Association for the Advancement of Health Education
1900 Association Drive
Reston, VA 22091
(703) 476-3437

Better Vision Institute
1800 North Kent Street
Rosslyn, VA 22209
(703) 243-1508

Center for Chronic Disease Prevention and Health Promotion
Centers for Disease Control
4770 Buford Highway, NE
Atlanta, GA 30341
(404) 488-5080

Choice in Dying
200 Varick Street
New York, NY 10014
(212) 366-5540

Consumer Information Center
18th and F Street, NW
Room G-142
Washington, DC 20405
(202) 501-1794

Food and Drug Administration
Office of Consumer Affairs
5600 Fishers Lane
Rockville, MD 20857
(301) 443-3170

National Institute on Aging
9000 Rockville Pike
Bethesda, MD 20892
(301) 496-1752

National Institutes of Health
9000 Rockville Pike
Bethesda, MD 20892
(301) 496-4000

National Wellness Association
1319 Fremont Street
South Hall
Stevens Point, WI 54481
(715) 346-2172

Office of Disease Prevention and Health Promotion
National Health Information Center
P.O. Box 1133
Washington, DC 20013
(800) 336-4797
(301) 565-4167 (in Maryland)

INDEX

BODY SYSTEMS: ANATOMY AND PHYSIOLOGY